Celebrate the Winter Holidays!

SENSATIONAL ACTIVITIES & BACKGROUND INFORMATION THAT HELP KIDS LEARN ABOUT AND APPRECIATE FIVE IMPORTANT HOLIDAYS

By Elaine Israel

HANUKKAH

CHRISTMAS

LAS POSADAS

KWANZAA

CHINESE NEW YEAR

SCHOLASTIC
PROFESSIONAL BOOKS

New York ✳ Toronto ✳ London ✳ Auckland
Sydney ✳ Mexico City ✳ New Delhi ✳ Hong Kong

Acknowledgments

Thank you, Darlene Cruse, Rochelle Eisenstein, Julio Muñoz, Gwen Parker-Ames, Terry Perkins, Raúl Rodriguez, and Iris Schwartz for reading my manuscript and sharing your holiday memories, recipes, and ideas. I am also most grateful to Connie Amend, and to Faye Boyes of the First Presbyterian Church of Burlingame, California, for allowing me to excerpt from its nursery school's excellent book, *The Twelve Months of Christmas*. And Liza Charlesworth—working with you is like having a holiday.

Developed by Raindrop Publishing LLC
Cover design by Kelli Thompson
Interior design by Debra Spindler
Interior illustration by Dana Regan
Edited and with contributions by Karen Kellaher and Janet Reed

Contents

For many years, my family lived on a wide avenue well-named the Grand Concourse. Every December, the YM-YWHA (Young Men's-Young Women's Hebrew Association) on the east side of the street would have a large Hanukkah menorah mounted on its facade. Directly across the street on the west side, a home for the aged had a big, bright Christmas tree on its terrace. The two symbols faced each other in harmony for all the winters of my growing up. For me, the facing images eventually came to symbolize the wonderful diversity of the neighborhood, New York City, and the nation.

Today, our country is even more diverse than it was back then. Children of all ethnic, racial, and religious backgrounds sit side by side in our schools. At no time is this more apparent than in early winter, when many religious and cultural groups are celebrating major holidays. While this diversity of customs makes some educators hesitant to teach about the holidays, other teachers find it a delightful challenge. Rather than ignore the holidays altogether, they teach about and celebrate as many holidays as possible. Such a curriculum helps students learn to respect the differences and similarities among various groups. It also lets every student in the class—regardless of background—feel represented and dignified.

This book gives you the tools you need to launch an exciting multicultural unit on the winter holidays. Here's hoping your unit is rich in learning experiences, uplifting moral lessons, and much joy.

Inside the Book

The book leads with a chapter to help you organize your holiday unit, including several culminating activities. Each subsequent section is about a different winter holiday: Hanukkah, Christmas, Las Posadas (a Mexican festival), Kwanzaa, and the Chinese New Year. Together, they add up to a complete theme unit that you and your class could cover in about three weeks, with each part taking about three days. Of course, there is enough material to last much longer, if you choose to make winter holidays an extended curriculum topic.

In each chapter, you'll find background information on the holiday, an explanation of its important symbols, plus age-appropriate activities to bring the celebration alive in your classroom. Activities include:

* Folk tales

* Mini-books to make and read

* Plays for the classroom

* Poems and songs

* Games and puzzles

* Recipes

* Crafts

* Cross-curricular activities

* Reproducibles

* Lists of age-appropriate books and Web sites

You may use the chapters in any order you like. One strategy would be to move through the holidays chronologically; another, to start with the holiday(s) your students seem most familiar with and move on to those that are new. However you choose to organize your unit, be sure to have fun!

Organizing Your Holiday Unit

Start your unit with a discussion of calendars and how they work. Understanding calendars will help students see why holidays happen when they do—and why so many take place in early winter.

Winter has always been a time for holidays. For thousands of years, almost every civilization has observed the winter solstice, the shortest day of the year. After the solstice, the days begin to grow longer again. Peoples of long ago held festivals to make sure the spring would come and the sun would chase away the darkness. The Druids carried blazing torches and held mysterious ceremonies in the shadows of their open-air stone temples. The ancient Romans held the *Saturnalia* celebrations in mid-December honoring Saturn, the god of plenty. At the end of the week, on December 25, came the Birthday of the Sun. Shops were closed and homes were decorated with wreaths of laurel leaves and gifts were exchanged.

Such solstice celebrations led to several modern holidays, including Chinese New Year, which is also known as the Spring Festival. Christmas, too, probably has connections to these celebrations. Although Christmas is a religious celebration rather than a solstice remembrance, many scholars believe that Christians in the fourth-century Roman Empire set the day at December 25 to coincide with Roman solstice celebrations that were taking place around them.

Some winter holidays are based on calendars other than the Gregorian one most people use today. For example, the date of Hanukkah is determined by the Jewish calendar, an ancient system based on the moon. This calendar is in use today in Israel, and by Jewish people around the world to calculate the times of religious observance. The Chinese use their own lunar calendar to determine the date for their New Year celebration.

Kwanzaa, which has its roots in African agricultural traditions, takes place at the time harvest festivals are held in Africa—from the middle of December to the beginning of January.

 Studying winter holidays gives us insights about people all over the world. We discover how alike many traditions are. Food is the most obvious example. Gift-giving is another common thread. So is the universal symbolism of candles and light. But the most essential quality the winter holidays share is an emphasis on community togetherness, caring, and responsibility. Amid the hoopla of the celebrations, it is important to remember why these holidays are observed. Happy Holidays!

LESSONS AND ACTIVITIES

Mark Your Calendar!

Bring in a large calendar to share with students. Discuss the months and seasons. Then explore the calendar by asking students to:

✳ Find their birthday months.

✳ Find their favorite holidays.

✳ Find some of the holidays in the theme unit. Christmas, Hanukkah, and Kwanzaa will probably be marked on the calendar. Las Posadas begins December 16. See page 94 for the date of the current Chinese New Year.

Afterward, students can have fun inventing new holidays, such as "I Love Chocolate Day," or "Play Outside Day." Encourage them to choose a date for their holiday, keeping in mind the appropriate season, and to describe how the holiday might be celebrated.

Where In the World?

As you study the holidays, keep maps handy. Mark each celebration's place of origin on the map as you go. Use a different-colored pushpin for each holiday.

Place	Holiday
Present-day Israel	Hanukkah and Christmas
China	Chinese New Year
Mexico	Las Posadas
United States and Africa	Kwanzaa

Languages Around the World

Studying holidays and cultures is a natural and fun way to introduce phrases from foreign languages. As you teach each holiday, introduce its greeting:

Hanukkah	Happy Hanukkah!	Hanukkah Same'akh! (Hebrew)
Christmas	Merry Christmas	Joyeuse Noël (French) Felíz Navidad (Spanish)
Las Posadas	Happy Posada	Felíz Posada (Spanish)
Kwanzaa	Happy Kwanzaa! Let's join together!	Kwanzaa yenu iwe heri! Harambee! (Swahili)
Chinese New Year	May you prosper! Happy New Year!	Gung Hay Fat Choy! Bai-nien! (Mandarin Chinese)

You can also teach holiday-related words such as "thank you" (*daw-jay* in Chinese; *gracias* in Spanish; *ahsante* in Swahili; *to-da* in Hebrew). Ask bilingual students, parents, and other community members to help you translate other words.

Holiday Talks
(Use with the reproducible on page 10.)

It's always interesting to learn about other cultures from firsthand information. Invite people from the community (including parents and students) to speak to your class about how they celebrate their holidays. If the visit includes cooking a special holiday treat or an arts and crafts demonstration, so much the better! Copy the simple interview guide on page 10 for older students; they can use the guide to ask questions of their visitors.

Bulletin Boards

An ever-changing holiday bulletin board is one way to get your class excited about the unit. Here are a few ideas: Visitor of the Week: Invite community members who celebrate each holiday to visit your class and talk about some of their favorite holiday traditions, stories, and foods. (See "Holiday Talks" activity, above.) Take a picture of each visitor. After each person's visit, post the picture, along with pertinent holiday facts and illustrations, on the bulletin board. Poetry Bulletin Board: Photocopy the poems and songs in this book and ask students to color the borders or illustrations. Cover a piece of cardboard larger than the page in wrapping paper and then attach the poem.

Book Link

For an excellent guide to common words and phrases in 15 languages (including Chinese and Spanish), consult Scholastic's *The Multilingual Translator* by Helen H. Moore (1994).

Numbers, Numbers!

Numbers are an important part of many holidays. Use these numbers for a daily math lesson while you're doing this holiday unit. Just for starters:

- ✷ the 8 days of Hanukkah
- ✷ the 12 days of Christmas
- ✷ the 4 weeks of Advent
- ✷ the 3 Wise Men

- ✷ the 7 days of Kwanzaa
- ✷ the 7 candles of Kwanzaa
- ✷ the 7 principles of Kwanzaa
- ✷ the 12 animals of the Chinese zodiac

Kindergarten students might simply write and illustrate the number (for example, write the number 7, then draw seven candles). With older students, toss out math puzzlers (for example, "How much longer is Hanukkah than Kwanzaa?").

Plan a Feast

(Use with the reproducible on page 11.)

No matter which holiday you celebrate, a feast is always in order. Throughout this book, you will find recipes and suggestions for authentic holiday treats. Put them all together, and you have the makings of a holiday food extravaganza! Designate a day toward the end of your theme unit as Feast Day, and start planning. If you have access to kitchen facilities, make the dishes together at school. If not, send the recipes home and ask parent volunteers to assist in preparing them.

What's a feast without guests? Ask children to make invitations for their families, caretakers, members of the school community, and visitors who have been part of your holiday unit. To make invitations, students can use the template on page 11. Just add the specifics and some colorful holiday illustrations! If you'd like, include a brief personal note, explaining what your unit has been about.

After the meal, try one or all of these enjoyable activities suggested by the First Presbyterian Church of Burlingame, California:

✳ Have cookie dough cut out and ready to decorate. (Make sure everyone has access to a hand-washing sink, soap, and paper towels.)

✳ On one table, place coffee cans and other tins with plastic lids that you've cleaned and collected during the year. Have stickers available to decorate the tins so they can be used as cookie tins.

✳ Ask volunteers to hold a puppet show or lead a sing-along.

Holiday Helpers

One thing all winter holidays have in common is a spirit of kindness and giving. Foster that spirit in your students by organizing a charity fundraising raffle. First, make a list of items your students could raffle off to the school community. Items might include:

✳ student-decorated, laminated placemats illustrating winter holidays

✳ small flowerpots decorated by your class

✳ photographs taken by a student, parent, or teacher

✳ students' framed original poems

✳ bookmarks designed and decorated by students

✳ sets of greeting cards made by students

✳ homemade baked goods in holiday shapes

✳ collections of recipes, including those in this book

Have the students select the charity to which you will send the raffle proceeds. If you'd prefer a non-monetary gift to the community, organize a class concert at a local nursing home.

Compare-and-Contrast Holiday Chart

As a culminating activity, create the chart on the board or on a large piece of paper. Read the questions aloud and have students provide the answers for you to fill in. Across the top, list the five holidays. Along the left-hand side, list questions about the holidays. Your chart will look something like the one below.

	Hanukkah	Christmas	Las Posadas	Kwanzaa	Chinese New Year
When is it?					
How long is it?					
Traditional food?					
Gifts exchanged?					
Where is it celebrated?					
How is it celebrated?					

Book Link

A wonderful book that provides an overview of dozens of world holidays is *Children Just Like Me—Celebrations* by Barnabas and Anabel Kindersley (DK Publishing in association with the United Nations Children's Fund, 1997). Each holiday is explained through the eyes of a child, via photos and captions. Have students look at the sections on Hanukkah, Christmas, and Chinese New Year. Ask: How are Isabel, Maria, and Man Po alike? How are they different? If you could meet one of these three children, who would it be? What would you ask?

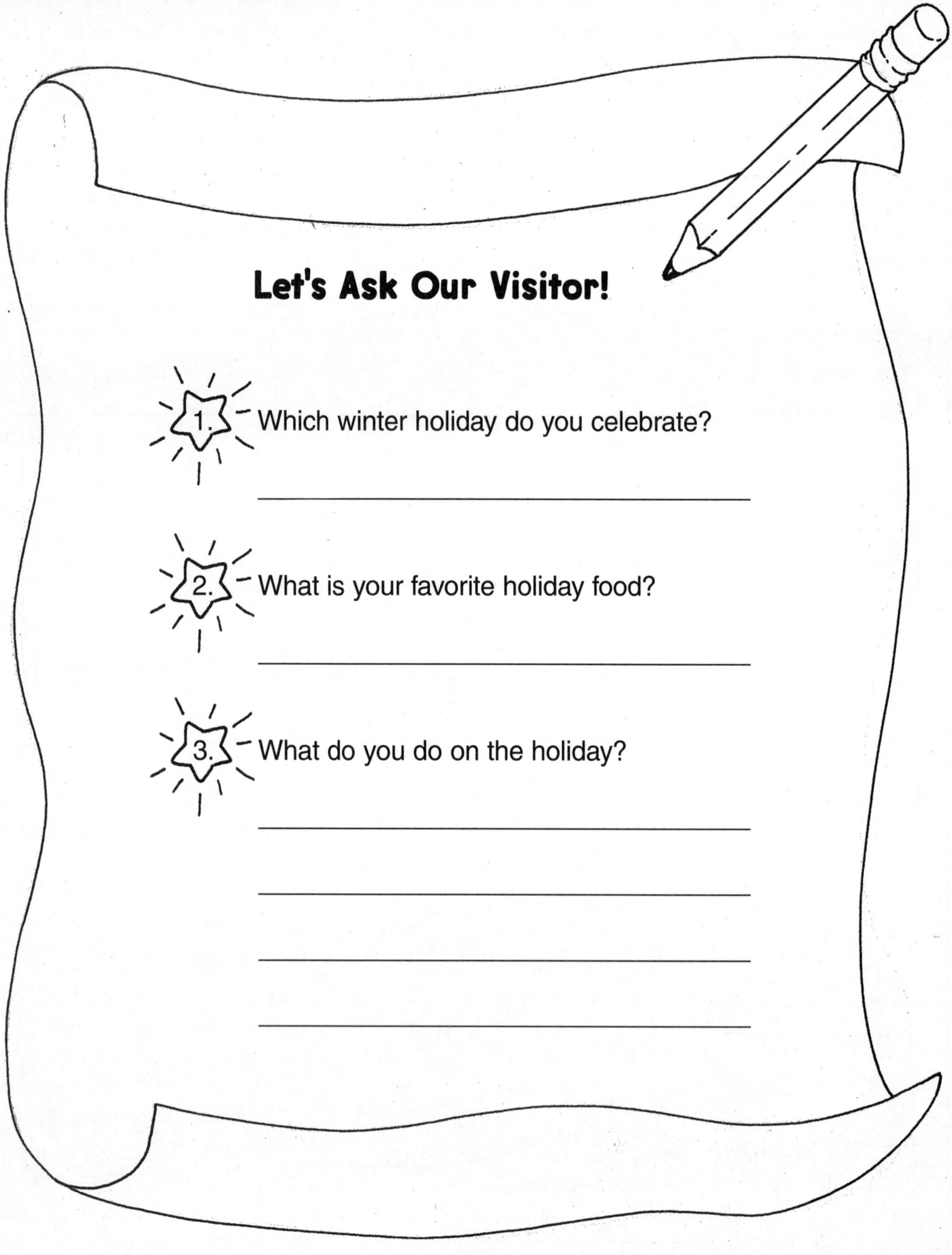

Let's Ask Our Visitor!

1. Which winter holiday do you celebrate?

_____

2. What is your favorite holiday food?

_____

3. What do you do on the holiday?

_____

_____

_____

_____

You Are Invited!

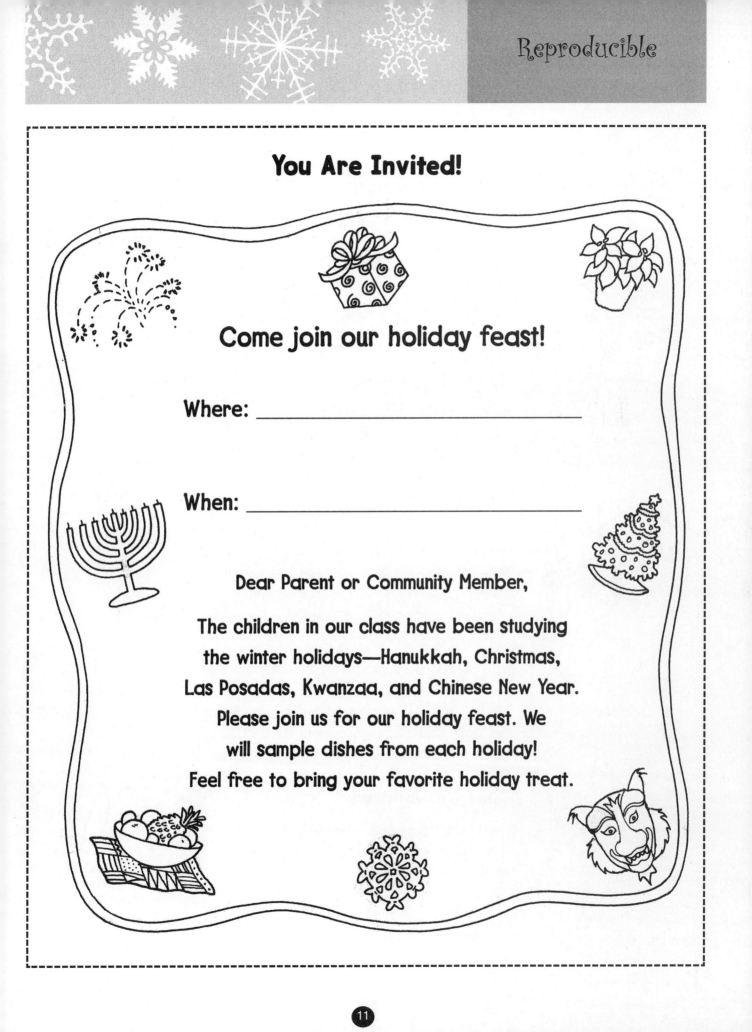

Come join our holiday feast!

Where: _____

When: _____

Dear Parent or Community Member,

The children in our class have been studying
the winter holidays—Hanukkah, Christmas,
Las Posadas, Kwanzaa, and Chinese New Year.
Please join us for our holiday feast. We
will sample dishes from each holiday!
Feel free to bring your favorite holiday treat.

See each chapter for an extensive list of resources related to each holiday.

Books for Teachers

All Around the Year: Holidays and Celebrations in American Life, by Jack Santino (University of Illinois Press, 1994).
Explores the history of American holidays.

Celebrations Around the World: A Multicultural Handbook, by Carole S. Angell (Fulcrum, 1996).
A wealth of information and activities for about 300 different holidays!

The Everything Christmas Book (Adams Media Corporation, 1996).
A potpourri of information mainly about Christmas, but also includes other holidays. There are songs, recipes, and crafts compiled by editors of this Massachusetts publishing house.

Family Traditions, by Elizabeth Berg (Reader's Digest, 1992).
Written from a warm, personal viewpoint and filled with general information.

Roots and Wings: Affirming Culture in Early Childhood Programs, by Stacey York (Red Leaf Press, 1991).
A valuable resource for educators who want to teach their students respect for all cultures. Includes activities to use in the classroom.

Books for Children

Children Just Like Me—Celebrations, by Barnabas and Anabel Kindersley (DK Publishing in association with the United Nations Children's Fund, 1997).
Join children all over the globe in celebrating important holidays.

The Story of Hanukkah

Hanukkah is a Jewish holiday that celebrates miracles. The story of Hanukkah begins more than 2,000 years ago. At this time, the Jewish people were living peacefully in Judea, part of a large kingdom including what are now Syria and Israel. As long as they followed the laws that the various rulers set, they were allowed to follow their religion.

But this changed. Two rulers, both named Antiochus, took power in turn. The first decided that his lands would be more secure if all citizens shared the same culture and religion. Unfortunately for the Jewish people, that meant praying to many gods rather than to the one God in whom they believed. Antiochus placed statues of gods everywhere, including the sacred Jewish Temple in Jerusalem. The second Antiochus carried this even further, finally sending his army to Judea. The army overran the land, killing anyone in its way. The Jewish people were unprepared for this terror. They were farmers, not soldiers.

Finally, a rebel band formed. It was led by a man named Mattathias Maccabee and his five sons. For three years, they faced down the stronger and better-equipped army. After Mattathias's death, his son Judah lead the rebels. Finally they triumphed, which was a miracle. Hanukkah celebrates another miracle as well. When the Maccabees reached Jerusalem and the Temple, they found its lamp. It had only enough oil for one day, but somehow it burned for eight days.

Hanukkah, also called the Festival of Lights, is a time to remember those joyous miracles. But the holiday has a sad side, too. Like the Maccabees, the Jewish people have faced great odds and survived. They endured and triumphed over centuries of horrific persecution. *Hanukkah* means *dedication* and is observed for eight nights beginning on the 25th day of the Hebrew month of *Kislev* (in November or December). On each night, a candle is lit in a special *menorah* called a *hanukkiah.* By the end of the holiday, nine candles will be blazing in the *menorah*—one for each night plus the *shamesh,* a "helper" candle that was used to light the others.

It has also become a custom to give and receive gifts at Hanukkah. Some families give one small gift on each of the eight nights. Others light the candles every night, but give gifts on only one.

Hanukkah Same'akh! Happy Hanukkah! (Note: Hanukkah is a Hebrew word with several acceptable English spellings. You may see the word beginning with the letters "Ch.")

Some Symbols of Hanukkah

 A menorah is a candleholder used in Jewish celebrations. It is the oldest Jewish symbol and the official emblem of Israel. A menorah usually holds seven candles. However, the special menorah used during Hanukkah holds nine—one for each of the eight nights of Hanukkah plus the candle which celebrants use to light the others.

Oil is an important Hanukkah symbol. It comes from the story of the great miracle in the Temple, when its oil lamp burned for eight days instead of one. Today, many traditional Hanukkah foods are fried in oil.

 A dreidel is a spinning top that Jewish children play with at Hanukkah. It has four sides, each with a Hebrew letter. The letters Nun, Gimmel, Heh, and Shin stand for the words "a great miracle happened there." One story for why children play with dreidels is that during the reign of Antiochus, Jews were forbidden to read the Torah. But, sometimes children would read the Torah anyway. If a soldier came along, the children would hide the Torah and pull out their spinning tops— pretending that they had been merely playing all along.

Some families place a tzedakah box in their home during Hanukkah. Tzedakah is the Hebrew word for justice. Family members put money in the tzedakah box to donate to charity.

 Many Jews give small sums of gelt, or money, as Hanukkah gifts. Children also receive coins made of chocolate. After the Jews battled the army of Antiochus and won their freedom, they began minting their own coins. It was a sign that they were truly free. Today, people exchange gelt as a celebration of that hard-won freedom.

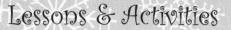 
The Hanukkah Miracle: A Classroom Mini-Play

(Use with the reproducible on pages 19-20.)

After you have shared with students the story of the great miracle of Hanukkah, read this mini-play that gives the story a modern-day twist. In it, a girl and her older brother encounter a Hanukkah miracle of their own. After giving away their last Hanukkah treat to a person in need, they find that there is still some left to share with their grandmother. Many early readers will be able to read the play on their own. With very young children, consider having a group of older children perform the play for your class. After students have read the play, have them compare the storyline to the story of the first Hanukkah. Then share some latkes with the class (see recipe on page 25)!

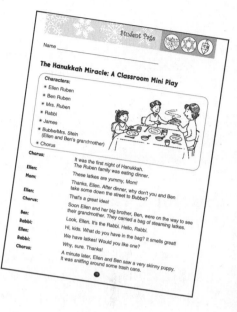

Happy Hanukkah (A Poem)

(Use with the reproducible on page 21.)

The poem "Happy Hanukkah" by Eva Grant conjures up warm moments of family togetherness. Distribute the poem and read it aloud to students. Then make up hand motions to follow with the rhyme. For example, students might wiggle their fingers in the air to represent falling snow in stanza one, or cup their ears to show children listening to a story in stanza two. After several readings, ask the children what they know about Hanukkah from the poem. (It's a winter holiday, it uses candles, etc.)

Dreidel, Dreidel

(Use with the reproducible on page 22.)

The first stanza of a favorite Hanukkah song is: "Dreidel, dreidel, dreidel. I've made you out of clay, and when you're dry and ready, then dreidel I will play." A dreidel (DRAY-del) is a four-sided spinning top made of clay, wood, plastic, or even heavy paper. Your students can play dreidel with simple handmade tops. Follow the instructions below.

<u>You Will Need:</u>
* copies of the reproducible on page 22 * heavy cardboard * pencils
* prizes (candy, pennies, or chocolate coins wrapped in gold foil) * glue

<u>What to Do:</u>
1. Divide the class into small groups. For younger students, reproduce and cut out enough of the dreidels so that each group has one. Older students should be able to cut them out on their own. Give each player the same number of pennies or candies.
2. Help students glue a dreidel pattern onto a "3 x 3" square of heavy cardboard. Make sure the letters N, G, H, and S appear on the sides of the square. Put a small hole in the center and place a medium-sized pencil through the hole. (The pencil may be sharpened or non-sharpened, but note that a sharpened pencil is not as safe and will leave pencil marks on the desktop when spun.)

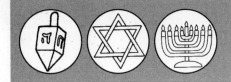
3. To start, have each student in each group put one prize in a pile in the middle. Have students take turns spinning the dreidel, following the rules of the game:

⁕ If the dreidel lands with the N (Nun) side up, the player does nothing.

⁕ If it lands with the G (Gimmel) side up, the player grabs all the prizes the middle.

⁕ If it lands with the H (Heh) side up, the player takes half of the prizes in the middle.

⁕ If it lands with the S (Shin) side up, the player must put one prize in the middle.

⁕ Before the next person spins, everyone must put another prize into the pile.

Color a Menorah
(Use with the reproducible on page 23.)

In some families, each person has his or her own menorah. Some are small and simple. Others are big and fancy. Reproduce page 23 for each student. Invite students to color in one candle on the menorah on each day of Hanukkah. (They can color the center helper candle along with the first night's candle.)

Hanukkah Match-Ups
(Use with the reproducible on page 24.)

To familiarize students with some of the special symbols of Hanukkah, have them play a matching game using the cards on page 24. Before starting, students should color the cards and discuss the name and meaning of each item (menorah, dreidel, Star of David, latkes, and a gift). Here's how to play.

Make It Harder

To make the game more challenging, make two copies of the reproducible and have students color the images so that each object has only one match. For example, they can color two of the menorahs red and two of them brown. In this version of the game, cards must be the same picture *and* the same color in order to be a match.

You Will Need:
⁕ a copy of page 24 for each pair of students
⁕ scissors

What to Do:
1. Divide the class into pairs. Have each pair color and then cut out the 12 cards.
2. Ask students to shuffle the cards without looking at them, and place them face down on the table or floor.
3. Players take turns looking for matches. At his or her turn, each turns over two cards. If the cards match, the student takes them. If the cards do not match, the student turn them back over.

The student should make sure the other player sees the cards before turning them back over. The winner of the game is the player with the most matches.

Rochelle's Delicious Latkes

(Use with the reproducible on page 25.)

At Hanukkah, one traditional food is latkes, or potato pancakes. Some families also eat jelly doughnuts. Both these foods are fried. The oil in which they are cooked represents the oil that kept the lamp in the Temple burning. Use the recipe to make latkes for your class. Or, send the recipe home for students to enjoy with their families. (Note: Since this recipe involves hot oil, it is recommended that adults handle the cooking part of this activity.)

Book Link When making or serving latkes to your students, read aloud *Latkes and Applesauce* by Fran Manushkin (Scholastic, 1990). In the book, snow has blanketed the trees and frozen the ground, forcing the Menashe family to give up their plans for a traditional Hanukkah feast of latkes and applesauce. But soon two unexpected visitors arrive and help the family find a way to enjoy their feast after all. After reading the tale, ask: How do you think Rebecca and Ezra felt at the beginning of the book? How do you suppose they felt at the end?

Hanukkah Promise Cards

(Use with the reproducible on page 26.)

You Will Need:

* 1 sheet of 9" x 12" construction paper
* patterns and Promise Certificate on page 26
* scissors * pencil * glue and paste, or tape
* crayons or markers * glitter

What to Do:

1. Reproduce and distribute page 26 to each child. Help children fill out the Promise Certificates. Then have them color the two patterns and cut them out. Set the Promise Certificate aside.

2. Fold the sheet of construction paper in half the long way.

3. Glue the dreidel pattern on one side. Glue the menorah pattern on the other side of the card.

4. Tape or staple the two short ends of the card along the edge. Leave enough space to put the Promise Certificate inside. Invite students to color and decorate their card with glitter.

5. Finally, slip the Promise Certificate inside the card.

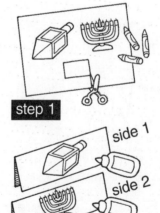

step 1

fold

step 2

side 1
side 2

step 3

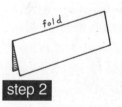
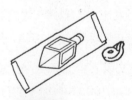

step 4

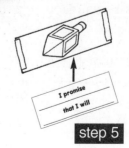

I promise _____ that I will _____

step 5

Justice Box

During Hanukkah, some families keep a "tzedakah box" in their homes. *Tzedakah* is the Hebrew word for justice, and a tzedakah box is a way of remembering those who are less fortunate. Families place money in the box during Hanukkah. Later, the money is given to charity. Because giving to the community is also a part of Christmas and Kwanzaa, a justice box is a wonderful way to tie these winter holidays together.

You can make a tzedakah box for your classroom using a shoe box and some everyday materials. Simply cover the box in wrapping paper or plain butcher paper and cut a rectangular hole in the top. If you use butcher paper, invite students to decorate the box with symbols of Hanukkah (and other holidays as well, if you are trying to tie them together).

Encourage students to donate coins to the box. After eight days, open it and see how much you've collected. Students can have fun counting the money by categorizing the change according to coin type. Once you have a total, ask students where they would like to donate their money. Have a few ideas ready in case they need inspiration! Some possibilities include local homeless shelters and soup kitchens, endangered-animal organizations, or the American Red Cross and other disaster-relief groups. Although your donation will likely be small, it's the spirit that counts! Involve children in writing a letter to your chosen charity to send along with the donation.

Hanukkah Crossword Puzzle
(Use with the reproducible on page 27.)

Most children love puzzles, and a crossword puzzle is a fun way to assess what students have learned during your Hanukkah unit. This one is so simple that even students who have never worked a crossword will be able to tackle it. There are no "filler" words; all of the answers relate to the celebration of Hanukkah. To avoid frustration, look over the crossword before distributing it and make sure you have covered all the answers.

Reproduce and distribute copies of the puzzle to your students. Show how the words can go across or down. Point out that they can skip a clue if it is tricky and come back to it later.

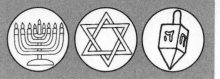

Name _____

The Hanukkah Miracle: A Classroom Mini-Play

Characters:

* Ellen Ruben
* Ben Ruben
* Mrs. Ruben
* Rabbi
* James
* Bubbe/Mrs. Stein
  (Ellen and Ben's grandmother)
* Chorus

Chorus:	It was the first night of Hanukkah. The Ruben family was eating dinner.
Ellen:	These latkes are yummy, Mom!
Mom:	Thanks, Ellen. After dinner, why don't you and Ben take some down the street to Bubbe?
Ellen:	That's a great idea!
Chorus:	Soon Ellen and her big brother, Ben, were on the way to see their grandmother. They carried a bag of steaming latkes.
Ben:	Look, Ellen. It's the Rabbi. Hello, Rabbi.
Rabbi:	Hi, kids. What do you have in the bag? It smells great!
Ellen:	We have latkes! Would you like one?
Rabbi:	Why, sure. Thanks!
Chorus:	A minute later, Ellen and Ben saw a very skinny puppy. It was sniffing around some trash cans.

Ellen:	Oh, look at that poor dog. He looks hungry!
Ben:	Let's give him a latke or two. That will fill him up.
Chorus:	Ellen and Ben were almost at Mrs. Stein's house when they heard a voice call out to them.
James:	Happy Hanukkah!
Ben:	Happy Hanukkah, James. Where are you going?
James:	I'm going to buy some food for dinner. My mom has been very sick. She could not make latkes for us this year.
Ellen:	Hmmmm. James, why don't you take some of these latkes home to your family?
James:	Really? Thanks a lot!
Ellen:	You're welcome.
Ben:	Oh no, Ellen. Now we have given away all of the latkes! The bag is empty!
Ellen:	I know Bubbe will understand.
Chorus:	They knocked at the door.
Bubbe:	Hello, children. I am so happy to see you! And what are you carrying?
Ellen:	It was a bag of latkes. But...
Bubbe:	They smell wonderful. Let me peek inside the bag. Oh, my! They look delicious, too!
Ellen:	They do? May I look? That's strange. Just a moment ago they were all gone!
Ben:	Maybe it's a Hanukkah miracle!
Bubbe:	Now come inside and share these latkes with me, and tell me all about this miracle of yours.

Name _____

Happy Hanukkah

Outside, snow is slowly, softly
Falling through the wintry night.
In the house, the brass menorah
Sparkles with the candlelight.

Children in a circle listen
To the wondrous stories told,
Of the daring Maccabeans
And the miracles of old.

In the kitchen, pancakes sizzle,
Turning brown, they'll soon be done.
Gifts are waiting to be opened,
Happy Hanukkah's begun.

by Eva Grant

From *Poetry Place Anthology* (Scholastic, © 1990)

21

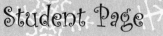

Dreidel Patterns

Color and cut out one dreidel pattern. Glue onto a 3" x 3" piece of cardboard. Put a pencil through the middle. Spin your dreidel!

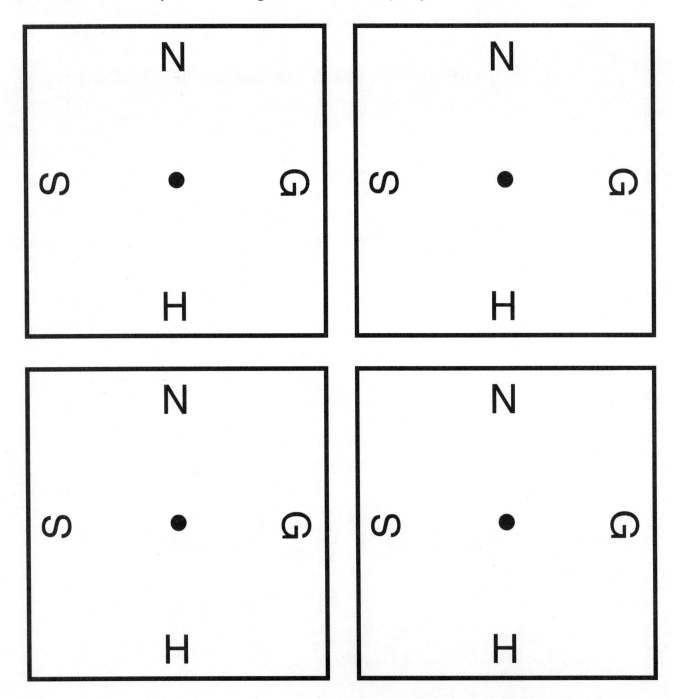

Name _____

Color a Menorah

Color one candle for each day of Hanukkah.

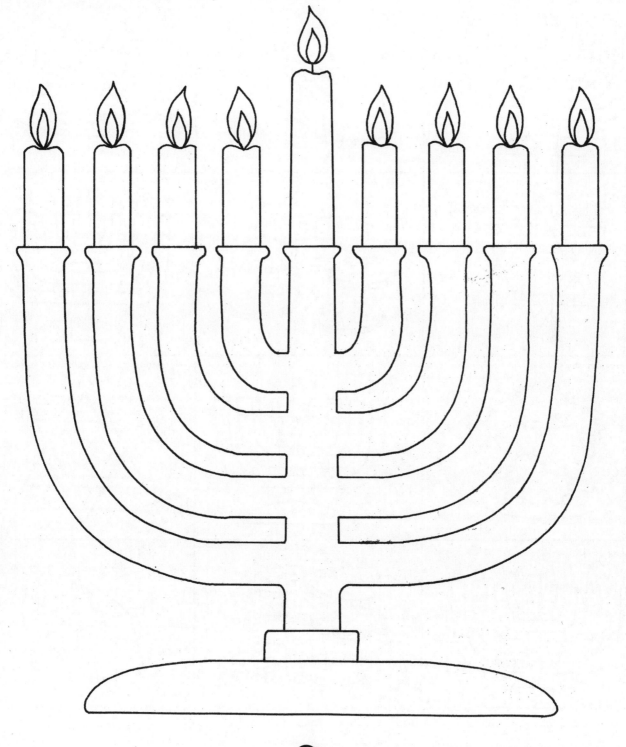

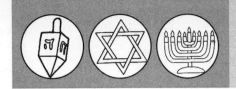
Name _____

Hanukkah Match-Ups

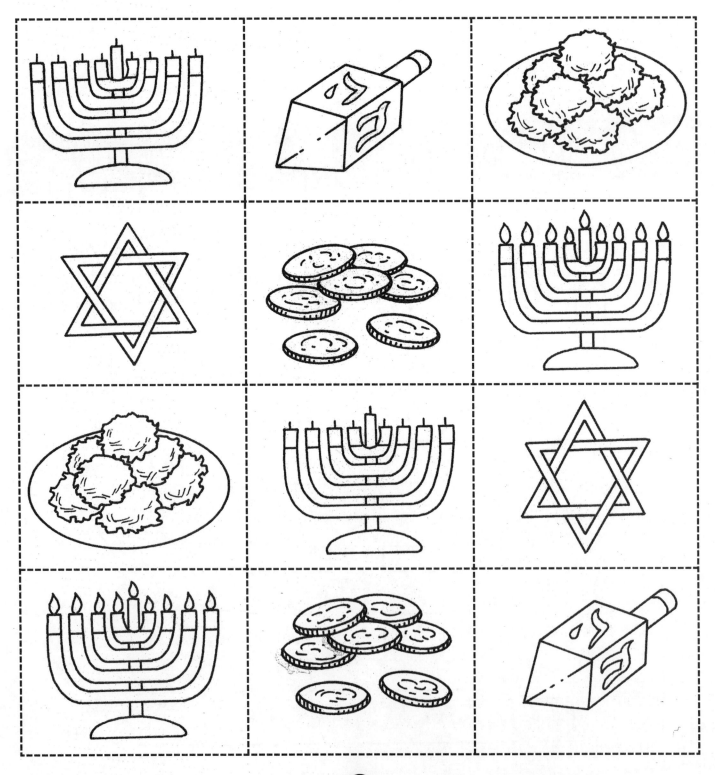

Name _____

Rochelle's Delicious Latkes
(Makes six servings)

You Will Need:

* 3 large potatoes (any kind, including sweet potatoes)

* 2 eggs

* 4 tablespoons grated onion

* 2 tablespoons matzoh meal or flour

* 1/4 teaspoon pepper

* 1 teaspoon salt

* vegetable oil

* 2 large bowls

* frying pan

* paper towels

What to Do:
(Grown-ups should handle all cutting and frying.)

1. Grate the potatoes but don't peel them.
2. Cover the bottom of a frying pan with vegetable oil.
3. In a bowl, cover the potatoes with water so they won't discolor.
4. Combine the onion, eggs, matzoh meal, and salt in a large bowl.
5. Remove handfuls of the potatoes from the water and squeeze them to remove all liquid.
6. Add the potatoes to the onions and eggs and mix well.
7. Place enough oil in the pan to cover the bottom. Cook on low to medium heat.
8. Place a heaping tablespoon of the mixture in the pan and spread it thinly.
9. Allow the batter to brown (about five minutes on each side).
10. Place on paper towels and drain. But don't cover the pancakes or they'll become soggy.
11. Keep the pan oiled as you add more batter.
12. Serve with sour cream or applesauce.

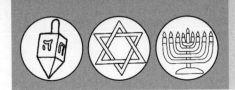

Name _____

Hanukkah Promise Card Patterns

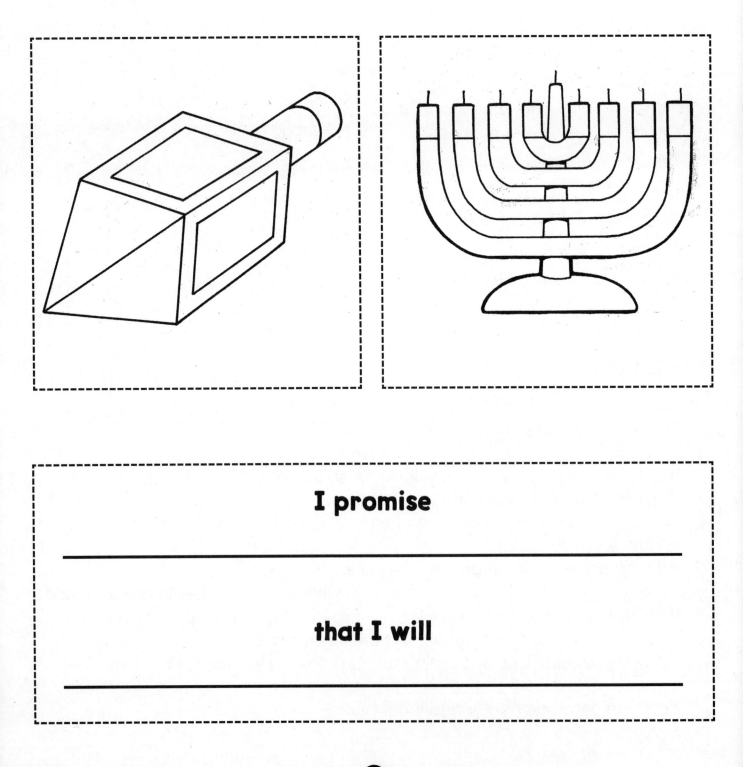

I promise

_____

that I will

_____

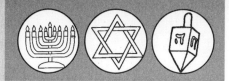

Name _____

Hanukkah Puzzle Time

Read each sentence below. Find the answer in the Word Box.
Write the answer in the crossword puzzle.

Word Box:

lights ✳ presents ✳ eight ✳ dreidel ✳ candles ✳ latkes

Across

1. During Hanukkah, children play

   with a _____ .

3. Hanukkah lasts for

   _____ nights.

5. During Hanukkah, people light

   _____ in a menorah.

6. Many people give and receive

   _____ during Hanukkah.

Down

2. Hanukkah is also called the

   Festival of _____ .

4. A special Hanukkah treat is

   _____ or potato pancakes.

27

Books for Children

Celebrate: A Book of Jewish Holidays,
by Judith Gross with illustrations by Bari
Weissman (Grosset & Dunlap, 1992).
   A slim paperback with explanations younger
   children can read and understand on
   their own.

Hanukkah!, by Roni Schotter with illustrations
by Mariylyn Hafner (Little, Brown, 1990).
   Celebrate along with five children and their
   family. The colorful illustrations are detailed
   and delightful.

A Hanukkah Treasury, edited by Eric A. Kimmel
with illustrations by Emily Lisker (Holt, 1998).
   This beautifully illustrated compilation includes
   stories, poems, songs, recipes, and crafts
   from such contributors as Jane Yolen and
   J. Patrick Lewis.

Inside-Out Grandma: A Hanukkah Story,
written and illustrated by Joan Rothenberg
(Hyperion Books for Children, 1995).
   Granddaughter Rosie gains a fresh
   perspective on Hanukkah as she listens
   to Grandma tell about past celebrations.
   The book also includes an interesting recipe
   for potato latkes.

The Menorah Story, written and illustrated
by Mark Podwal (CIP, 1998).
   Clear text and lovely pictures tell the story
   of how the menorah came to be.

Poems for the Jewish Holidays, selected
by Myra Cohn Livingston with illustrations by
Lloyd Bloom (Holiday House, 1986).
   Not just for Hanukkah, the poems are
   illustrated with lyrical black-and-white art.

The Tie Man's Miracle, by Steven Shnur
with illustrations by Stephen T. Johnson
(Morrow Junior Books, 1995).
   This bittersweet story about Mr. Hoffman,
   the tie seller, and Seth, a boy eager to get
   on with Hanukkah celebrations, is perfect
   for all ages.

On Hanukkah, by Cathy Goldberg Fishman
with illustrations by Melanie Hall
(Atheneum, 1998).
   A girl and her family celebrate the
   Festival of Lights in this informative and
   poetic picture book.

Latkes and Applesauce, by Fran Manushkin with
illustrations by Robin Spowart (Scholastic, 1990).
   When a blizzard strikes during Hanukkah,
   a family still manages to find a way to enjoy
   their traditional holiday meal.

Books for Teachers

*Chanukah: Eight Nights of Light;
Eight Gifts for the Soul*, by Shimon Apisdorf
(Leviathan Press, 1997).
   A book to help families remember
   the real meaning of the holiday.

Web Sites

www.childfun.com/themes/holidayz.html
   Fun classroom activities relating to Hanukkah
   and more than a dozen other holidays.

The Story of Christmas

Christians around the world celebrate Christmas as the birth of Jesus, whom they believe is the son of God. The holiday is celebrated every year on December 25.

The story of Christmas is told in the New Testament of the Bible. According to the Bible, Jesus was born about 2,000 years ago to a woman named Mary. Mary was told by an angel that she was carrying the son of God. Toward the end of her pregnancy, Mary and her husband, Joseph, traveled from their home in Galilee to Bethlehem, the home of Joseph's family, in order to be counted in a census. When the couple arrived in Bethlehem, they could find no place to stay. They finally took shelter in a stable, and there, among the farm animals, Mary gave birth to the baby Jesus. An angel appeared to shepherds in a nearby field and announced that the savior had been born. The shepherds went to see the baby, as did three kings who came bearing gifts. The kings followed a star to find the stable.

The exact birth date of Jesus is not known. However, early Christians wanted to set aside a special day to remember the Nativity. In the fourth century, the pope established the date December 25. The name "Christmas" is a combination of the religious service known as the "Mass" and "Christ": Christ's mass.

Today, Christmas is celebrated by two billion Christians worldwide. On this special day, they attend church services and gather with family and friends at home. Other customs vary by country. For example, in France, children set out their shoes on Christmas Eve for a figure named Père Noël (Father Christmas) to fill with gifts. In Germany and Scandanavia, families burn a yule log.

 Here in the United States, families exchange presents, decorate Christmas trees, sing carols, and share a feast. Adding to the excitement is the arrival of Santa Claus, who comes to children's homes on Christmas Eve and leaves toys and gifts for them to open on Christmas Day. The legend of Santa Claus became part of Christmas celebrations in the nineteenth

century, and is actually rooted in fact. In the fourth century, a bishop named Nicholas distributed money and gifts to children and the poor. Nicholas later became a saint and the inspiration behind the Santa story. Merry Christmas!

Some Symbols of Christmas

 The custom of decorating a Christmas tree has ancient roots. Hundreds of years ago, evergreen trees symbolized the promise of springtime—the promise that the barren winter landscape would once again become green. In the fifteenth century, people began decorating their homes with evergreen leaves and branches at Christmastime. Later, people began decorating whole trees.

 Stars are often placed on the top of Christmas trees, and appear on wrapping paper, and decorations. The star stands for the star that guided the three kings to the stable where Jesus was born.

 Angels are also frequently seen as Christmas images representing the angel who appeared to the shepherds to announce the birth of Christ.

Many Christians display Nativity scenes made of clay, wood, or other materials. These figurines of Mary, Joseph, the baby Jesus, the shepherds and the kings help celebrants remember the story of Christmas.

Advent is the four-week season of preparation for Christmas that begins on the Sunday closest to November 30. An Advent wreath is a circle of evergreen branches with four large candles, one to be lighted on each Sunday of Advent. The candles represent Jesus, who said, "I am the light of the world."

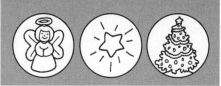

Silver Cones for Christmas: *A Mini-Book to Make and Share*

(Use with the reproducibles on pages 37-40.)

Legends about Christmas abound. In some parts of the world, it is said, barn animals speak on Christmas Eve. Other tales have to do with the fir tree, which has been called the Tree of Life. In this activity, your students will make a mini-book centering on a Christmas legend from the Harz Mountains in Germany. In this heart-warming story, a poor mining family receives the Christmas gift of a lifetime. Before making and reading the mini-books, show children a map of Europe, pointing out Germany. Then have the children follow the steps below to create their books. Read the tale aloud, inviting students to follow along in their own mini-books.

Spiced Pine Cones

After reading the story, ask children to help you make fragrant pine cones for your classroom.

You Will Need:
* opened pine cones
* spices, such as cloves, nutmeg, and cinnamon
* glue

What to Do:
1. Working on one side of the cone, put a drop of glue on each tip.
2. Sprinkle the spices onto the wet glue and let dry.
3. Repeat on the other side of the cone.

HOW TO MAKE A **MINI-BOOK**

You Will Need:
* double-sided copies of pages 37-38 and 39-40
* crayons or markers

1. Copy the reproducible pages 37-38 and 39-40 on standard 8.5" x 11" paper. Make the copies double-sided.

2. Fold the front cover/back cover in half along the dotted line.

3. Fold the inner pages in half along the dotted line.

4. Place the inner pages inside the cover, keeping the page numbers in correct order. Staple the edge to bind the book.

5. Have students color their illustrations. Then invite them to share their mini-books with their families.

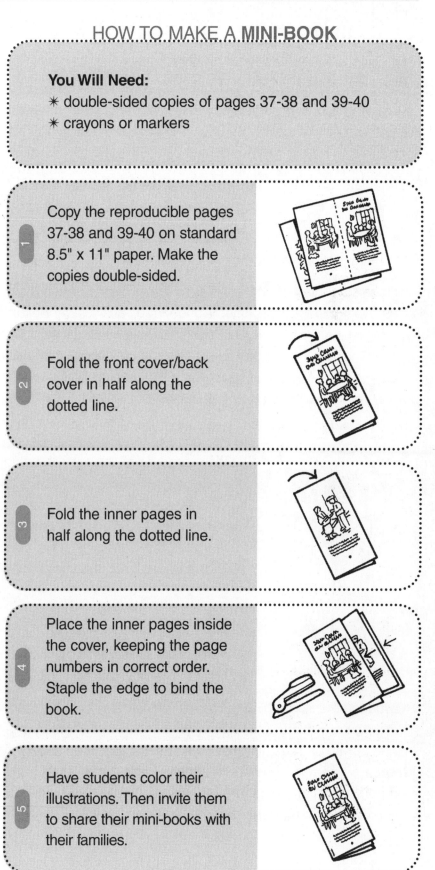

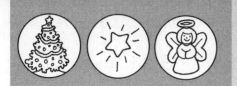

A Time for Giving: A Classroom Mini-Play
(Use with the reproducibles on pages 41-42.)

This mini-play is about a group of children who are looking beyond the commercial meaning of receiving gifts. It is a perfect way to get students started thinking about sharing their talents and skills with others.

Make copies of the mini-play found on pages 41-42 and help your students perform it several times, so that all students have a chance to play the major roles. Those not performing can be part of the audience and join in singing the chorus of "Deck the Halls" at the end of the play.

After the play is performed, talk with the class about what they can do to spread the holiday spirit. Some suggestions include:

✳ Have students perform the play for other classes. Hold a sing-a-long of popular holiday songs such as "Deck the Halls," "Winter Wonderland," and "Jingle Bells." You may wish to ask your students to bring in a CD or tape of his or her favorite holiday music. Or you may want to provide a cassette recorder or CD and play popular and classical musical selections such as, "Tchaikovsky's "Nutcracker Suite," or something of Bach's or Handel's.

✳ In the "spirit of giving" have students make holiday cards for all the school "helpers," who are often forgotten. People such as the librarian, the lunchroom staff, the school nurse, and so on. You also may wish to include community helpers that have visited the class or that the class has visited, such as firefighters or police officers.

A Rhyme for the Season
(Use with the reproducible on page 46.)

Reproduce the poem "Everywhere Is Christmas" for each student. Read the poem aloud and discuss it with your class. The poem conveys the idea that Christmas is celebrated just about everywhere—in places with fir trees, in places with palm trees, atop snowy mountains, and in flat corn fields. Ask: Where do you see signs of Christmas? Have the children make a collective list of everywhere they see signs of Christmas in the days and weeks leading up to the holiday: store windows, city streets, school hallways, even in their own living rooms!

Distribute copies of the poem. On the other side of the paper, invite students to draw pictures of what Christmas looks like in their neighborhoods or homes. Do families hang lights outside their homes? Does the town have a Nativity display? Is the Christmas season snowy and cold or sunny and warm? Children will have fun incorporating these details into their Christmas scenes.

To Grandma's House We Go: A Christmas Board Game

(Use with the reproducibles on pages 43-45.)

The Christmas season often feels hectic, even to children. Take a breather by having pairs of students play this simple board game. The game lets children celebrate Christmas traditions (singing carols and telling Christmas stories) while moving toward a finish line. To play, make copies of the instructions and the game board for each pair of students. Show students how to tape the game together. Provide two pennies to each pair. Finally, read and review the directions so that students can play independently.

Under the Christmas Tree: A Class Collaborative Book

(Use with the reproducibles on pages 47 and 48.)

If your students love hearing holiday stories, imagine their reaction to hearing one they've authored themselves! By following the instructions below, your class can make a fun "lift-the flaps" book about the spirit of giving. Have each student create one page, then compile the pages into a collaborative book.

You Will Need:

✳ one copy of page 47 and 48 for each student ✳ crayons or markers
✳ a 9" x 12" sheet of construction paper ✳ tape ✳ glue ✳ scissors

Book Link

Before working on your collaborative book, read *The Jolly Christmas Postman,* by Janet Ahlberg and Allan Ahlberg (Little, Brown, 1991). As students read about the postman delivering holiday gifts, they'll become eager to create their own gift story.

What to Do:

1. Distribute a copy of page 47 and 48 to each student. Show students the blank line in the rhyme where they should write their name. Ask students to cut out the tree and glue it onto a piece of construction paper, making sure to place the tree high enough so the gift box can fit underneath.
2. Read the rhyme aloud, and explain that they will draw a present under the tree. It should be a gift they would like to give to a loved one—a parent, grandparent, sibling, friend, or other special person. Emphasize that the imagined gifts need not be store-bought; a student might choose to give a parent a coupon promising to set the table, or a younger sibling an hour of play-together time. (But don't worry if students can only come up with ideas for store-bought gifts; at least they are in the spirit of giving.)

3. Help students fill in the line at the bottom explaining what the gift is and whom it is for.

4. When students have finished their "gifts," have them color their gift boxes and cut both of them out. Then have them glue their gift beneath the tree. Help them place the box on top of their gift illustrations. Put a strip of tape along the top edge of the gift box, creating a flap that students will open to see the picture underneath.

5. Compile the pages in any order. Use a piece of construction paper to create a cover for the book. Use the title, "Under the Christmas Tree," or another of your own choosing. Bind the book together with staples, or punch holes in the pages and bind them with yarn or ribbon.

6. Read the collaborative story aloud. Pause before opening each flap, so that students can guess what each classmate placed under the tree. Remind the student who created that page to keep mum!

Other Fun Foods for Christmas

Sugar cookies
Made in the shapes of angels, stars, trees, etc. You can roll out store-bought dough and let students do the decorating!

Popcorn
Eat some and use the rest to decorate the room!

Cider, Please!
(Use with the reproducible on page 49.)

In England and other European countries, it's a Christmas tradition to serve hot mulled cider to carollers who come to the door. This tasty drink is a wonderful way to warm up on a cold December day. It's also easy to make, even if you don't have cooking facilities in your classroom. (Chances are, your school cafeteria staff won't mind you warming the cider in their kitchen, especially if you offer them a cup!) Consider making cider for your students to sip as they work on other holiday projects, or send the recipe home for families to enjoy together.

Bottle-Cap Wreaths

Wreaths are used as decorations throughout the Christmas season. They are usually made of evergreen branches. Evergreen trees, which remain green all year long, have always been a sign to people that spring would come again. Your students can make their own wreaths with all sorts of everyday materials. Here's one fun project that uses caps from soda pop, juice, and water bottles!

You Will Need:
* used, washed bottle caps * styrofoam plates or sheets of cardboard * green yarn
* white glue * spray paint or craft paint

What to Do:
1. Help students cut a wreath shape out of heavy cardboard. Or cut the center out of a large foam plate.
2. Show students how to wind green yarn around the shape.

3. Then have students paint bottle caps with appropriate colors.

4. Help students glue the caps on the yarn wreaths.

Get creative! In addition to bottle caps, you might try decorating your wreaths with dried flowers, holly leaves cut out of paper, macaroni dyed with food coloring, and cotton balls.

Trim-a-Tree Treasure Hunt

(Use with the reproducible on page 50.)

Every Christmas tree is unique. Many families have treasured ornaments that have been passed down through generations or handmade by members of the family. In this activity, students hunt for specific decorations hidden in a Christmas tree illustration. The activity is an excellent way for students to practice visual discrimination and to explore the tradition of decorating a Christmas tree.

Distribute the reproducible and challenge students to find the items mentioned in the clue. Have students color in the items as they locate them. Afterward, invite students who celebrate Christmas at home to talk about (or even bring to school) ornaments that are meaningful to their families. Just be sure each ornament gets back home safe and sound! (An alternative would be to have the students draw a special ornament for homework, then tell about it in class the next day.)

The Twelve Days of Christmas: A Countdown Calendar

(Use with the reproducibles on page 51-53.)

The Twelve Days of Christmas is the period that falls between Christmas Day, December 25, and Three Kings' Day, January 6. According to the Bible, it took the three kings (also known as the three magi, or three wise men) twelve days to reach Bethlehem after hearing of Jesus's birth. Three Kings Day is the celebration of their arrival. In some countries, people even exchange gifts on Three Kings Day instead of on Christmas. Since many schools are closed between Christmas and New Year's Day, you might time the activity for the twelve days leading up to Christmas, or even earlier in the holiday season.

This countdown calendar offers a small, enjoyable activity for each of the twelve days of Christmas. All are things that students can do on their own, either at school or at home. Some are as simple as jokes and tongue twisters; others are slightly more involved. You can create one countdown calendar for the whole class to use (invite one student to open the calendar each day and read the activity aloud), or have each student make his or her own calendar.

You Will Need:

✳ a copy of pages 51-53 for each calendar you are making ✳ an empty egg carton for each calendar (foam or cardboard) ✳ scissors ✳ red and green tempera paint, paintbrushes

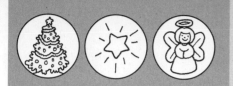

What to Do:

1. Paint the egg carton red. Let it dry.
2. Turn the carton upside down. Use the green paint to paint the numbers 1 through 12 on the egg cups. Follow this pattern:

1	2
3	4
5	6
7	8
9	10
11	12

3. Once all the paint has dried, cut the top of each egg cup about halfway off.
4. Cut out the twelve activities from the reproducible. Fold them and put one in each egg cup.
5. For twelve days in a row, open one cup and follow the suggested activity.

No Time?

You can simplify the countdown calendar by omitting the paint. Simply use a marker to write the numbers 1 through 12 on a plain carton. Or simplify even further by putting the activities in a hat or bowl and letting students pull out one activity each day.

No-Bake Ornaments

Once students have explored the story and traditions of Christmas, they will enjoy making clay ornaments of their favorite Christmas symbols. These ornaments are not difficult to make (no baking involved!) and make perfect classroom decorations or gifts for family members. If you do not have access to a stovetop at school, prepare the clay in advance and bring it in an airtight container.

You Will Need:

✳ 1 1/2 cups water ✳ 2 cups salt ✳ 1 cup cornstarch ✳ spoon ✳ cookie cutters in shapes of Christmas symbols ✳ rolling pin ✳ waxed paper ✳ drinking straws ✳ tempera paint and paintbrushes ✳ red and green ribbon ✳ scissors

What to Do:

1. Boil the water in a saucepan. Remove the pan from the heat and add the cornstarch and salt. Stir.
2. Put the pan back on low heat, and stir until thick.
3. Put the mixture on a large piece of waxed paper. Allow the mixture to cool.
4. Knead the mixture, then use the rolling pin to roll it out.
5. Cut shapes in the mixture with cookie cutters.
6. Use the straw to poke a hole in the top of each ornament.
7. Let the ornaments dry for 3 days, then paint them.
8. Slide a piece of ribbon through the hole on each ornament. Tie the ribbon and use it to hang the ornament.

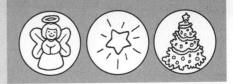

8

The miner's wife knew the valuable silver was enough to see her family through many a hard day and cold night. The elf had given her the best Christmas present ever.

Silver Cones for Christmas

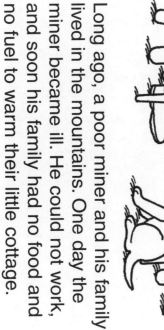

1

Long ago, a poor miner and his family lived in the mountains. One day the miner became ill. He could not work, and soon his family had no food and no fuel to warm their little cottage.

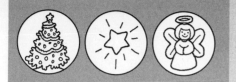

Inside the cottage, the wife poured the pine cones onto the table. She couldn't believe her eyes! Each of the cones was made of pure silver.

7

The miner's wife thought of a way to earn money. She would collect pine cones from the woods and sell them for people to burn as fuel.

2

6

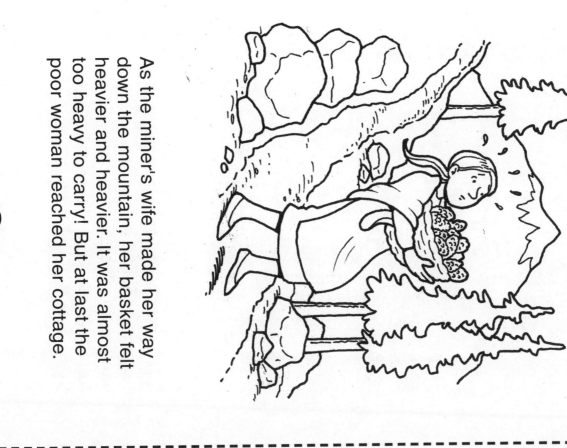

As the miner's wife made her way down the mountain, her basket felt heavier and heavier. It was almost too heavy to carry! But at last the poor woman reached her cottage.

3

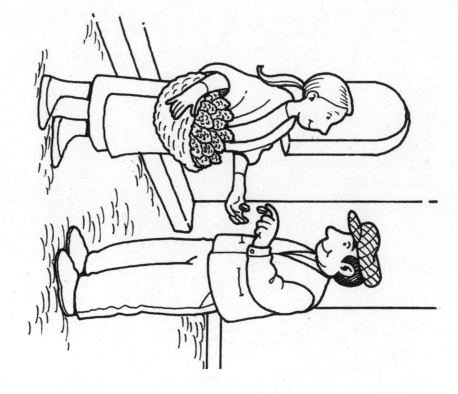

Every day, the miner's wife climbed the mountain and brought down as many pine cones as she could carry. She sold them and made just enough money to buy a little food for her family.

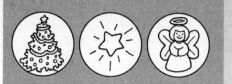

The miner's wife thanked the elf and began to pick up the cones. As she worked, hundreds more began to fall from the tree. She filled her basket to the brim.

5

One day just before Christmas, an elf jumped out from behind a fir tree, surprising the miner's wife as she worked. "Take only the cones from under this tree," the elf said. "They are the best."

4

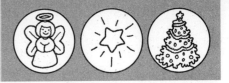

Name _____

A Time for Giving: A Classroom Mini-Play

Characters:

* Narrator 1   * Max
* Narrator 2   * Diane
* Teacher   * Tim
* Emily   * Rob
* Sarah   * Julie
* Lindsay   * Jayson
* Ben

Fa-la-la-la-la-la-la-la-la

Narrator 1:	It was the week before Christmas.
Narrator 2:	Rehearsal for the class play was over.
Children:	(Sing refrain from "Deck the Halls": Fa-la-la-la-*la*-la-la-la-*la*!)
Teacher:	Good work. The holiday play is on Thursday. Don't forget your costumes.
Sarah:	This is going to be fun.
Ben:	Maybe we'll get into the Christmas spirit at last.
Diane:	What do you want for Christmas?
Max:	Computer games.
Emily:	CD's.
Tim:	Me too.
Lindsay:	But I don't really need anything.
Rob:	Me neither.

Julie:	How can we make this Christmas special?
Narrator 1:	The children thought about it.
Narrator 2:	Then Lindsay spotted a poster on the wall. (The children look at an imaginary poster.)
Lindsay:	Look what this poster says.
Sarah:	"Christmas is a time of giving."
Max:	It has some great ideas.
Jayson:	Collect canned foods for the soup kitchen.
Emily:	Do something for others.
Tim:	We need a giving project.
Diane:	Collect toys for kids in need.
Rob:	I have toys to give!
Lindsay:	So do I!
Max:	Me too!
Sarah:	What else?
Ben:	We could help with the used-clothing drive.
Julie:	We could sing carols at the hospital!
Jayson:	This is what Christmas is about.
Children:	(Sing refrain from "Deck the Halls": Fa-la-la-la-*la*-la-la-la-*la*!)

Name _____

To Grandma's House We Go Game Directions

How fast can you get to Grandma's house for Christmas dinner? Play this game with a classmate and find out.

<u>You Will Need:</u>

✳ the game board

✳ 2 players

✳ different-color buttons, paper clips, or other objects to use as playing pieces

✳ 2 pennies

<u>How to Play:</u>

1. Place your playing pieces on Start. Decide who will go first.

2. Flip both pennies. If you get two heads, move one space. If you get two tails, move two spaces. If you get a head and a tail, move three spaces.

3. Follow the instructions in the box you land on. If the box is empty, your turn is over.

4. The player who reaches Grandma's house first is the winner!

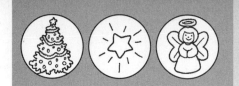

To Grandma's House We Go Game Board

Start

Traffic jam, go back to Start.

Stop to buy wrapping paper, go back 1 space.

Grandma's House

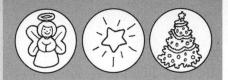

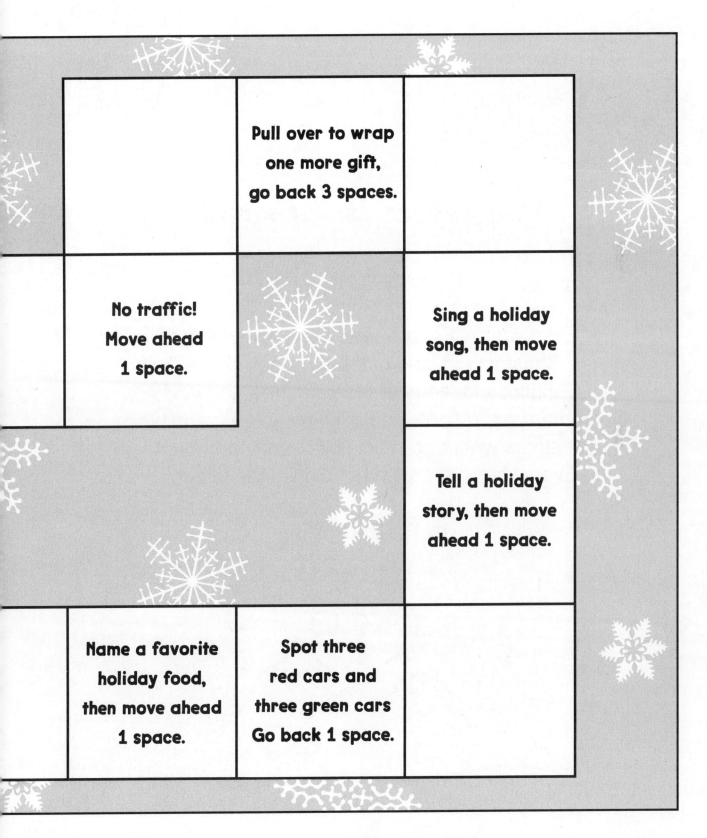

Pull over to wrap
one more gift,
go back 3 spaces.

No traffic!
Move ahead
1 space.

Sing a holiday
song, then move
ahead 1 space.

Tell a holiday
story, then move
ahead 1 space.

Name a favorite
holiday food,
then move ahead
1 space.

Spot three
red cars and
three green cars
Go back 1 space.

Name _____

Everywhere Is Christmas

Everywhere. Everywhere, Christmas tonight!
Christmas in land of the fir tree and pine,
Christmas in lands of the palm tree and vine,
Christmas where snow peaks stand solemn and white,
Christmas where corn fields lie sunny and bright,
Everywhere, everywhere, Christmas tonight.

by Phillip Brooks

From *1001 Christmas Facts and Fancies*,
by Alfred C. Hottes (Dodd, Mead, 1933)

Name _____

Under the Christmas Tree Pattern

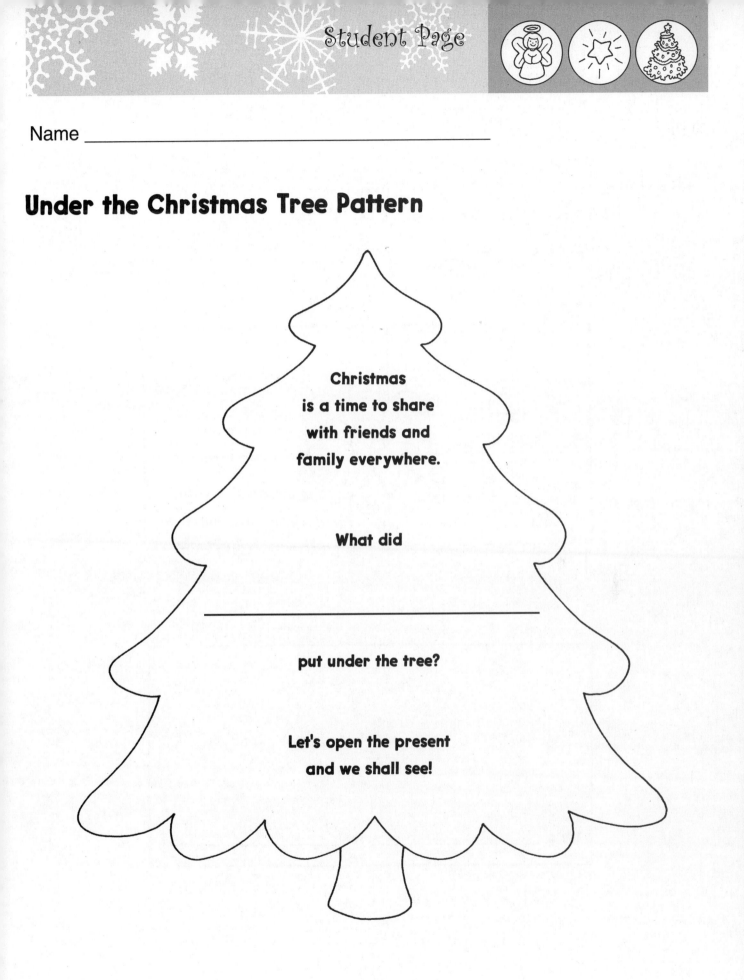

Christmas
is a time to share
with friends and
family everywhere.

What did

_____

put under the tree?

Let's open the present
and we shall see!

Name _____

Under the Christmas Tree Patterns

It's a _____ for _____!

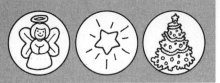

Name _____

Warm Mulled Cider

You Will Need:

* apple cider (8 ounces for each student)

* cinnamon sticks, 2-3 inches long (two per student)

* whole cloves

* sugar

What to Do:

(Children should have a grown-up's help.)

1. Pour the cider into a large saucepan.

2. For each cup of cider add one clove, one cinnamon stick, and one teaspoon sugar to the saucepan. Bring to a boil.

3. Remove the saucepan from heat and let cool for several minutes (cider should be warm but not boiling hot).

4. Ladle the cider into mugs or foam cups. Add a stick of cinnamon to each cup.

Name _____

Trim-A-Tree Treasure Hunt

Can you find an angel and three little stars,

A tiny toy trumpet and an old-fashioned car,

A teddy bear and two big bows,

And Christmas lights in four neat rows?

Can you find a candy cane and a bell,

A little goldfish and an old seashell,

A house and a sled and a penguin, too?

I can see them all! Can you?

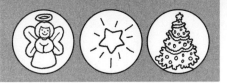

Name _____

The Twelve Days of Christmas

Cut out the cards. Use them in your Countdown Calendar.

Day 1

Say Merry Christmas in Spanish (Felíz Navidad!) and French (Joyeuse Noël!).

Day 2

Take a survey of your friends and family to learn their favorite holiday foods.

Day 3

Name five words that rhyme with tree. Use them to write a Christmas poem.

Day 4

Share this riddle with a friend:

Why is Christmas like a lion at the beach? (Answer: Both have sandy claws!)

The Twelve Days of Christmas (continued)

Cut out the cards. Use them in your Countdown Calendar.

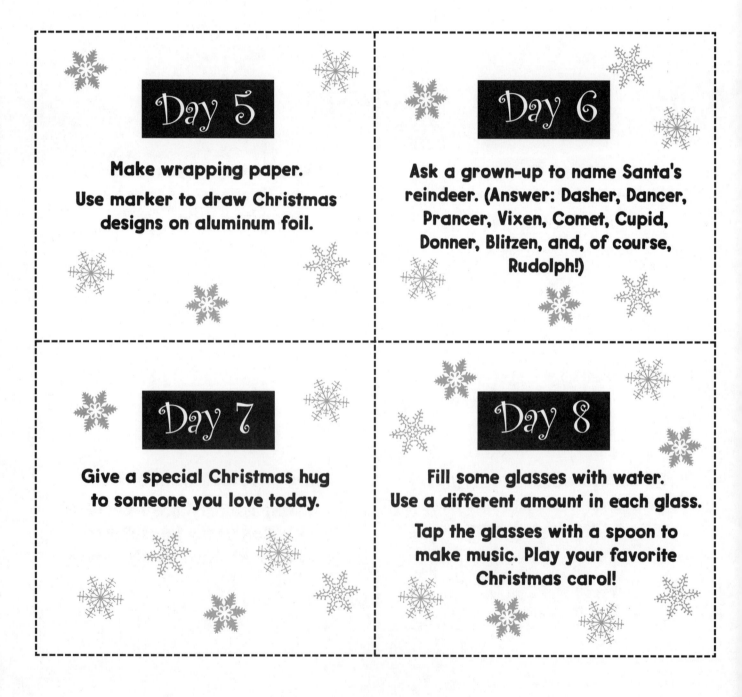

Day 5

Make wrapping paper.

Use marker to draw Christmas designs on aluminum foil.

Day 6

Ask a grown-up to name Santa's reindeer. (Answer: Dasher, Dancer, Prancer, Vixen, Comet, Cupid, Donner, Blitzen, and, of course, Rudolph!)

Day 7

Give a special Christmas hug to someone you love today.

Day 8

Fill some glasses with water. Use a different amount in each glass.

Tap the glasses with a spoon to make music. Play your favorite Christmas carol!

The Twelve Days of Christmas (continued)

Cut out the cards. Use them in your Countdown Calendar.

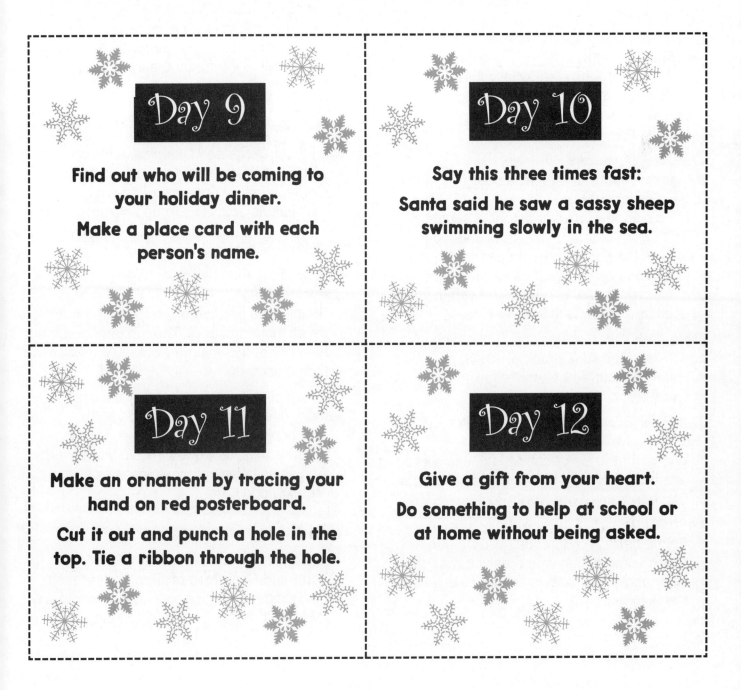

Day 9

Find out who will be coming to your holiday dinner.

Make a place card with each person's name.

Day 10

Say this three times fast:

Santa said he saw a sassy sheep swimming slowly in the sea.

Day 11

Make an ornament by tracing your hand on red posterboard.

Cut it out and punch a hole in the top. Tie a ribbon through the hole.

Day 12

Give a gift from your heart.

Do something to help at school or at home without being asked.

Books for Children

The Christmas Day Kitten, by James Herriot
(St. Martin's, 1986).
> A dying stray cat leaves her kitten
> with the person she most trusts. This
> bittersweet story, like all those by the
> English country vet, is heartwarming and
> memorable.

It's Christmas, by Jack Prelutsky
(Greenwillow, 1981).
> Kids need poetry—especially if it's
> written just for them. This collection
> has selections for several holidays,
> but consider it a Christmas gift.

The Jolly Christmas Postman,
by Janet Ahlberg and Allan Ahlberg
(Little, Brown, 1991).
> Here's another rhyming story, a sequel to
> The Jolly Postman. The Christmas book
> follows the postman as he delivers
> Christmas cards. Each has a small gift
> enclosed, so this is a book to keep in your
> desk and share with special care.

Olive, the Other Reindeer, by J. Otto Siebold
and Vivian Siebold (Chronicle, 1999).
> Here's a picture book that's fun
> for all ages.

The Polar Express, by Chris Van Allsburg
(Houghton Mifflin, 1985).
> Winner of the Caldecott Medal, this classic
> relates the fantasy of a boy riding the Polar
> Express train to the North Pole.

Merry Christmas, Strega Nona,
by Tomie dePaola (Harcourt, 1986).
> Learn some Italian words as you read this
> story about Big Anthony and his surprise
> Natale feast.

Tree of Cranes, by Allen Say
(Houghton Mifflin, 1991).
> The author illustrates this book with
> exquisite watercolors to tell the story
> of a boy and a unique Christmas
> celebration in Japan.

The Twelve Days of Christmas,
by Jan Brett (Dodd, Mead, 1986).
> This may seem like the same old, same
> old, but this lovingly presented version is a
> great way to introduce the traditional song
> to children.

Books for Adults

Christmas Crafts and Customs,
by Virginia Fowler (Prentice-Hall, 1984).
> Craft-lovers will find dozens of fun
> multicultural activities to do with kids, from
> French Christmas crowns to Filipino
> Christmas stars.

Kids' Holiday Fun, by Penny Warner (Simon &
Schuster, 1994).
> Simple arts and crafts, recipes, and more
> for all major holidays. Though intended for
> family use, the volume works just as well in
> the classroom.

Christmas Around the World, by various
authors (New Orchard Editions, 1985).
> This book includes music, paintings, folk
> tales, recipes, as well as the story of the first
> Christmas taken from the Gospels of
> Matthew and Luke.

Web Sites

www.christmas.com
> You'll find Christmas recipes from around
> the world, decoration ideas, and how to say
> "Merry Christmas" in many languages.

The Story of Las Posadas

Las Posadas is celebrated in Mexico from December 16 to December 24. Although Las Posadas (lahs-poh-SAH-dahs) is part of the Mexican celebration of Christmas, it is also a vibrant festival in and of itself, with many unique traditions and symbols.

As mentioned in Chapter 2, Christmas is a time when Christians celebrate the birth of Jesus. Part of the Christmas story is Mary and Joseph's search for lodging in Bethlehem. There was no room at the inn, so the weary couple took shelter in a small stable, where Jesus was born. On each of the nine nights of Las Posadas (*posada* is Spanish for "inn"), Mexicans reenact the Holy Family's search for shelter. Groups of children walk through their neighborhoods. They go from house to house, carrying small figures of Mary and Joseph. At each home, the children knock on the door and ask for lodging. Each time, the children are told there is no room. Finally, after trying several houses, the children are invited into a home for a pre-arranged party.

Posada parties are often held each night of the festival. Some Posada parties are held in private homes; others take place in town centers or church halls. At each party, there is food, drink, and games for the children. The most popular Posada game is breaking a piñata full of candy and trinkets.

During Las Posadas, many children enjoy dressing up as Mary, Joseph, the magi, shepherds, and barn animals. They carry candles or lanterns to light their way, and sing carols or blow whistles as they walk. On Christmas Eve, the last night of the festival, children carry a small figure of the baby Jesus in addition to the figures of Mary and Joseph. When they are invited in for the party, they place the figure of Jesus in a manger in the host family's *nacimiento,* or nativity scene.

Felíz Posada! Happy Posada!

Some Symbols of Las Posadas

Children carry lanterns called faroles or candles to light their way during the Posada processions.

During Las Posadas, families display a *nacimiento,* or nativity scene, in their homes. The nacimiento is often passed down through generations and is given a prominent spot in the home. The manger holding the baby Jesus is left out of the nacimiento until Christmas Eve.

Mexican families decorate their homes with poinsettia plants at Posada time. There are several Mexican legends about this flower, which blooms in mid-December. According to one tale, a young boy was visiting his village church and felt badly that he did not have a gift to place before Jesus in the church nativity set. The boy grabbed some branches of a plain green plant that was growing by the side of the road. Before the boy's eyes, the plant's green leaves turned a vibrant red.

No Posada celebration would be complete without a piñata. Made of clay and papier maché, the piñata is filled with candy, nuts, and little trinkets. At a Posada party, children take turns trying to break the piñata with a stick. When it finally breaks open, the children grab the treats and gifts. Piñatas can take any shape, including simple balls and stars, but they are often shaped like animals.

Room at the Inn: A Classrom Mini-Play

(Use with the reproducibles on pages 61-62.)

One way to make Las Posadas come alive for students who have never experienced it is to act out the celebration in your classroom. Distribute copies of the mini-play to your students and read it aloud once to the class. Then assign roles and have students themselves read the lines, if possible. Although the play can be performed while students are at their seats, you may enjoy creating props and having the children perform "on stage" in your classroom. Draw three houses on sheets of posterboard, and have a small group of students stand behind each house. The houses should be scattered throughout the room. The other students can knock on the door of each house as they proceed through the classroom. If your students are not yet reading, consider asking an older class at your school to perform the play for your class.

Point out to students that in a real Posada celebration, the children would be speaking Spanish, and that the children's and neighbors' lines would probably be sung instead of recited.

Spanish-English Spinner

(Use with the reproducibles on pages 63-64.)

Children seem to have a natural talent for and curiosity about languages. While exploring Las Posadas with your class, take some time to introduce some simple Spanish words. Because the festival lasts for nine nights, introducing the numbers one through nine makes a great starting point.

In this activity, students will construct spinners that match numerals with corresponding Spanish words. To assemble the spinners, follow these simple directions:

You Will Need:
✳ a copy of page 63 and 64 for each student ✳ a brass fastener for each student ✳ crayons or markers for coloring the spinners ✳ scissors

What to Do:
1. Have students cut the circle from each page.
2. Then have them cut the two small windows out of the cover. (Students will need assistance with this step.)
3. Place the cover on top of the inside spinner. Push the brass fastener through the center of both circles. Open and flatten the legs of the fastener so the two circles stay in place.
4. Turn the cover until the number 1 appears in the bottom window. Look at the top window. Point out that "uno" is the Spanish word for "one." Continue turning the cover until students have seen and said all of the numbers in Spanish.

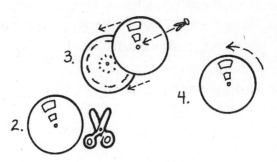

Find the Posada Party!

(Use with the reproducible on page 65.)

To reinforce the Las Posadas theme of searching for lodging, distribute copies of page 65 and invite students to navigate the maze. As students work their way through the maze, they will collect letters, ultimately spelling out the Mexican word for "party" (fiesta).

Other Fun Foods for Posada

Tamales
sweet dough wrapped inside corn husks

Empanadas
meat filling inside a pastry shell

Buenos Buñuelos!
A Posada Recipe to Make and Share

(Use with the reproducible on page 66.)

Posada celebrations are a time to savor rich Mexican foods. One favorite dish is buñuelos, which are sweet Mexican pancakes. Follow the recipe on page 66 to make two dozen servings of this tasty treat. You can prepare the dish at home and warm it in the microwave in the school cafeteria, or send the recipe home for students and families to prepare together.

Poinsettia Prints

During Las Posadas, Mexican homes and stores are filled with bright poinsettia plants. These flowers, known worldwide, are native to Mexico. They bloom once a year, in early December. Your students can make their own beautiful poinsettia prints.

You Will Need:
* red, yellow, and green tempera paint * black marker
* clean, dry kitchen sponges * butcher or construction paper

What to Do:
1. Show students a live poinsettia or some pictures from cards, magazines, or books.
2. Draw a poinsettia flower on the board.
3. Have students use markers to draw leaves on kitchen sponges. Use one sponge for each leaf and make the leaves as large as possible.
4. Cut out the leaf shapes.
5. Use the sponges to stamp a picture of a poinsettia on the paper. Dip one sponge-leaf in red paint to stamp the star-shaped flower. (You will need to dip several times.) Then dip another sponge leaf in green paint and stamp green leaves all around the red ones. For the inside of the red flower, use a scrap of sponge to make small red and yellow dots.

Before or after making the poinsettia prints, you may want to share this Mexican legend with your class:

The Poinsettia Gift

A long time ago, on the night before Christmas and the last night of Las Posadas, a little boy decided to visit the church in his village. In the church there were statues of Mary, Joseph, and the baby Jesus. The boy wanted to bring a gift to Jesus, but he had no money. On his way to church, the boy saw some green plants growing by the side of the road. "Aha!" he thought. "I will pick some plants and bring them to Jesus." And so the boy pulled some green plants from the earth. As he did, an amazing thing happened. The green leaves of the plant turned a beautiful shade of red! The boy continued on to the church and placed the plants before the statue of Jesus. At that moment, a bright star appeared in the sky above the village. It was the brightest star anyone had ever seen. "It is a night for miracles," said the little boy. And that is how the beautiful poinsettia came to be. People in Mexico call it the *flor de la noche buena*, or Christmas Eve flower.

Pinata Fun

Celebrate Las Posadas with a handmade piñata! In Mexico, piñatas are usually made from clay molds. However, this piñata activity uses a balloon mold. It is easier to make and safer to use in or around school.

<u>You Will Need:</u>
* a balloon * wallpaper paste * newspapers * string or twine * paint
* small candies and trinkets * long stick or broom handle * blindfold

<u>What to Do:</u>
1. Blow up the balloon. Keep it round rather than elongated. Choose one part of the balloon to be the piñata top.
2. Cut two very long pieces of string or twine. Wrap each piece around the balloon as you would wrap a ribbon around a gift. Tie both strings at the piñata top (the spot you chose in step 1). Leave the ends of the string long.
3. Tear the newspaper into long strips.
4. Protect your desk or table with extra newspaper. Begin dipping the newspaper strips in the paste and placing them on the balloon. Have students help cover the balloon in four or more layers of newspaper. Leave a 3" diameter circle at the piñata top. Do not put newspaper on this circle, because you will need it to fill the piñata.
5. Let the newspaper dry.
6. Pop the balloon.
7. Paint your piñata however you'd like.
8. Fill the piñata with candy, trinkets, or other small treats. Do not use heavy items.
9. Hang your piñata using the dangling string or twine. Blindfold children and have them use a stick or broom handle to break the piñata open.

Where Is Mexico?

As you explore Las Posadas, point out that Mexico is a close neighbor of the United States. (In fact, many Las Posadas traditions have made their way into the U.S.) Help students locate Mexico on a map and identify the capital (Mexico City). You might also wish to share some of these interesting facts:

✳ Most Mexican people are *mestizos,* of mixed Spanish and Native American ancestry.

✳ The long, narrow piece of land below Mexico is called Central America because it connects North America and South America. (Mexico is part of North America.)

✳ Mexico has several active volcanoes.

Las Posadas Comes to School

Act out the Las Posadas tradition of going door to door searching for shelter. Ask other teachers in your school if your students can knock on their classroom doors during the reenactment. Supply them with the correct response when students beg for lodging ("No, there is no room here.") Then plan a party in the school gymnasium or in a classroom. On the day of the reenactment, have students carry unlighted candles as they walk through the halls. Invite other classes to join your Posada party.

What Happened Next?

(Use with the reproducible on page 67.)

Challenge students' higher-order thinking skills with the sequencing activity on page 67. The four squares show a family selecting and using a piñata during Las Posadas. By paying close attention to the details in the illustrations, your students should be able to put the squares in the correct order. If you'd like, have them cut out the squares to do the sequencing activity. Afterward, invite the children to make up text to go with the pictures. They'll have their very own short story about a family preparing a Las Posadas piñata.

Name _____

Room at the Inn: A Classroom Mini-Play

Characters:
* Miguel
* Rosalita
* Carlos
* Maria
* Neighbor 1
* Neighbor 2
* Neighbor 3
* Chorus

Miguel: Hello, friends. It is December 16.
Do you know what that means?

Rosalita: Tonight we celebrate Las Posadas!

Miguel: That's right. What time shall we gather?

Carlos: Let's meet here at seven o'clock.

Maria: I can hardly wait!

Chorus: That night the children met and began walking.
After a while, they stopped at a house.
Knock, knock.

Neighbor 1: Yes?

Maria: Can you help us? We need lodging for the night.

Neighbor 1: Go away. There is no room here.

Chorus:	And so the children kept walking until they came to another house. Knock, knock.
Neighbor 2:	Yes?
Carlos:	We need someplace to stay. Can you give us a room?
Neighbor 2:	No, I am sorry. We have no room.
Chorus:	The children walked a little farther, until they came to a third house. Knock, knock.
Neighbor 3:	Who is it?
Rosalita:	We are looking for lodging.
Neighbor 3:	Our house is full.
Rosalita:	Please. We are very tired. Can't you help us?
Neighbor 3:	Come in. We will find room.
Chorus:	The children walked into the house. A party was waiting for them.
Miguel:	This tamale is delicious!
Maria:	So is this candy I got from the piñata!
Rosalita:	Happy Posada, everyone!
Chorus:	Happy Posada!

Name _____

Spanish-English Spinner – Cover

Name _____

Spanish-English Spinner—Inside

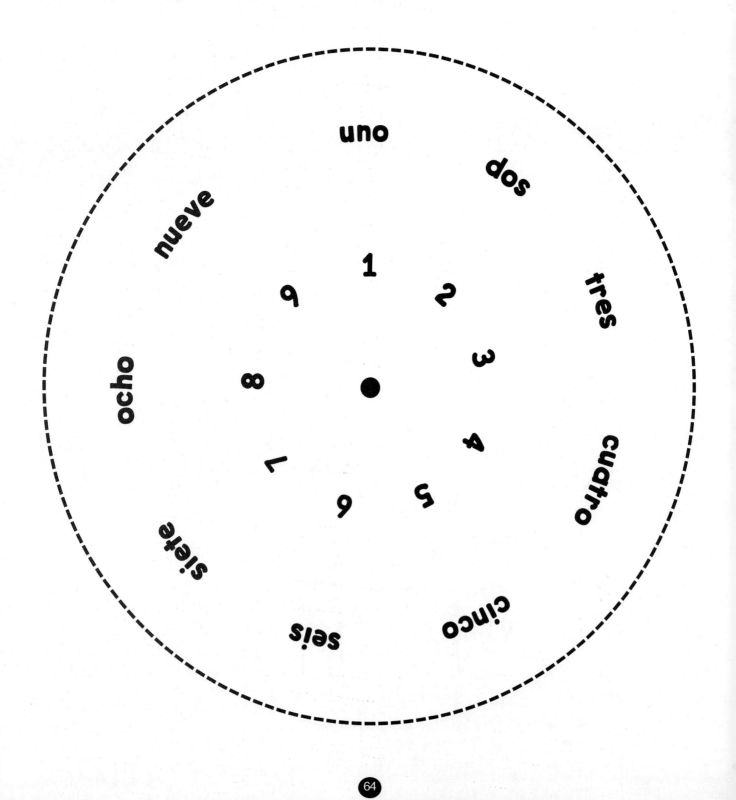

Name _____

Find the Posada Party!

Can you help the children find the Posada party? Work your way through the maze. Circle all the letters along your path as you go. On the correct path, the letters will spell out the Mexican word for "party"!

Name _____

Buñuelos Recipe

Here's an easy recipe for the delicious Las Posadas favorite, buñuelos, or fried sugar tortillas. Make sure you work with an adult.

You Will Need:

* 3/4 cup milk
* 1/4 cup butter or margarine
* 2 eggs
* 3 cups all purpose flour
* 1 teaspoon baking powder
* 1 teaspoon salt
* cooking oil
* brown sugar
* maple syrup
* saucepan
* bowl
* frying pan

What to Do:

(Grown-ups should handle all heating and frying.)

1. In a saucepan bring milk and butter to a boil. Let cool.
2. Beat the eggs and then stir into saucepan mixture.
3. In a bowl, stir flour, baking powder, and salt together.
4. Add mixture and mix well until you have dough.
5. Knead dough 2 or 3 minutes or until smooth.
6. Shape the dough into 20 balls. Let stand 5 minutes.
7. Press each ball into a 4" circle.
8. In a frying pan, heat cooking oil (375 degrees).
9. Carefully place the tortillas into the oil. Turn them once. Cook about 4 minutes or until brown.
10. Drain tortillas on paper towels.
11. Sprinkle brown sugar on tortillas, add syrup, and enjoy!

Name _____

What Happened Next?

Look at the pictures. Help put them in order.
Write a number—1, 2, 3, or 4—in the boxes inside each picture.

Books for Children

Christmas in Mexico, by Cheryl L. Enderlein (Hilltop Books, 1998).

An easy-to-read chapter book tells the story of Las Posadas and other MexicanChristmastime traditions.

Books for Teachers

The following books were actually written for older students (fourth grade and up), but make excellent teacher resources and are suitable for reading aloud.

Christmas in Mexico, by Corinne Ross (World Book, 1976).

Includes lyrics and music for several Las Posadas songs!

Fiesta!, by Elizabeth Silverthorne (Millbrook Press, 1992).

This book details Mexican holidays throughout the year and includes several mouth-watering recipes.

Fiesta Time in Mexico, by Rebecca B. Marcus and Judith Marcus (Garrard Publishing, 1974).

Lively and detailed text helps readers experience Las Posadas and a handful of other holidays.

Web Sites

www.inside-mexico.com/Revista.htm

A newsletter describing Las Posadas and other Mexican Christmas customs.

The Story of Kwanzaa

E ach year, from December 26 to January 1, thousands of African-American families celebrate Kwanzaa, a modern cultural festival with roots in Africa's traditional harvest celebrations. Kwanzaa is a time for those whose ancestors came from Africa to rejoice in their values and honor their heritage. The seven days of Kwanzaa are bittersweet; they recall not only the blessings of a good harvest, but also the painful experiences of slavery, racism, and oppression.

Despite its traditional roots, Kwanzaa is a fairly new holiday. It was created in 1966 by Dr. Maulana Karenga, an African-American professor and political activist. The 1960s were years of great social change in the United States and were defined for many people by the Civil Rights movement. Dr. Karenga was inspired by the marches, demonstrations, and peaceful protests he saw taking place. But he was also aware that his community needed to remember the past. He created Kwanzaa as an opportunity for African-Americans to recall their collective experiences—both in Africa and in America—and to dedicate themselves to the good of the community. He chose the dates of Kwanzaa to coincide with late-December African harvest festivals.

The name *Kwanzaa* comes from the phrase *matunda ya kwanza,* which means "first fruits" in Swahili, a widely-spoken African language. Dr. Karenga added an extra *a* to the word *kwanza* so that it would have seven letters. The number seven is meaningful because Kwanzaa lasts for seven days, and because each day of the festival centers on one of seven important principles: unity, self-determination, collective work and responsibility, cooperative economics, purpose, creativity, and faith. During

Kwanzaa, families, friends, and neighbors come together to remember each of these seven principles. They decorate their homes with special symbols, wear traditional African clothing, light candles in a *kinara,* share stories, perform skits, exchange gifts, and drink from a Unity Cup. The festival usually wraps up with an elaborate *karamu,* or feast, featuring traditional African-American dishes.

Tens of millions of people now celebrate Kwanzaa, but the holiday's newness means that it is still being defined. Each family, each group of friends and neighbors, brings a unique slant to its Kwanzaa celebration. However, all Kwanzaa celebrations have a common purpose—to celebrate the unity and heritage of the African-American community.

Kwanzaa yenu iwe heri! Harambee! Happy Kwanzaa! Let's join together!

The Symbols of Kwanzaa

Celebrants drink a toast from a *kikombe cha umoja,* a Unity Cup.

The kinara is a candle holder. It holds one candle for each of Kwanzaa's seven days.

The candles in the kinara are called the *mishuma saba.* They are placed from left to right in this order: three red candles, one black candle, and three green candles. The black candle in the center is lit first. One candle is lit every night. Red, black, and green are the colors of the African-American flag.

✳ Red stands for the blood black people shed.
✳ Black stands for unity and the face of African-American people.
✳ Green stands for hope and is the color of Africa, the motherland.

Mazao (mah ZAH o) are crops, such as fruits and vegetables. They are placed on the table during the Kwanzaa celebration.

The *mkeka* (em KAY kah) is a straw mat. It represents tradition. The intricate patterns woven through the mkeka have been passed down from generation to generation in Africa and in America.

Vibunzi (Vee-BUNZ-ee) or, *muhindi* (moo-HIN-dee) is corn. At least one ear of corn is placed on the mkeka for each child in a family. The corn represents hope for the future.

When families celebrate Kwanzaa, they often exchange gifts, truly special gifts that are made by hand. If children have made and kept promises during the year past, adults reward them with presents. A typical gift is a book or a symbol of the black heritage, such as a piece of *kente* cloth. Children, too, give gifts. The Swahili word for gifts is *zawadi.*

Lessons & Activities

Explore the Seven Principles

Each of the seven days of Kwanzaa is dedicated to one of seven principles. In Swahili, these are known as the *nguzo saba.* Each day of Kwanzaa, introduce one principle to your students. Invite older children to think of examples of that principle at work in their everyday lives (some examples are given below). With very young children, focus on a few principles that are easy for them to understand (creativity, unity), and ask kids to draw pictures illustrating each principle.

English	Swahili
Unity	Umoja
Self-determination	Kujichagulia
Collective work and responsibility	Ujima
Cooperative economics	Ujamaa
Purpose	Nia
Creativity	Kuumba
Faith	Imani

What the Principles Mean:

Day 1/December 26
Unity: We join together as a family, as a community, and as a nation.
Example: You are kind to your brothers and sisters in order to help keep your family strong and happy.

Day 2/December 27
Self-determination: We speak up for ourselves and plan our own futures.
Example: You decide to become a teacher because you know you can do it. You don't let others talk you out of it.

Day 3/December 28
Collective work and responsibility: We work together to solve problems.
Example: After a neighbor's home burns down, your community chips in to provide lodging, clothes, and food for the family.

Day 4/December 29
Cooperative economics: We support African-American stores and businesses.
Example: You decide to buy your groceries at a corner store run by a neighbor, rather than go to a large supermarket chain.

Day 5/December 30
Purpose: We choose a goal and work toward it little by little.
Example: You promise to be more helpful at home—then, each day, you choose one job to do (setting the table, cleaning your room, listening the first time you are asked to do something).

Lessons & Activities

Day 6/December 31

Creativity: We use all of our own talents and appreciate the talents of others.

Example: You sing a song to your baby brother, or read the poems of great African-American poets.

Day 7/January 1

Faith: We believe in our parents and community leaders. We believe that African-Americans will win the struggle for equality.

Example: You don't feel bad about yourself, even if someone tries to treat you differently because of your skin color.

Gifts for Kwanzaa

Gift-giving is a part of many winter holidays, and Kwanzaa is no exception. Kwanzaa gifts are usually handmade and have special meaning for both the giver and receiver. Here are some ideas for meaningful gifts your students can prepare, whether they actually celebrate Kwanzaa at home or are simply learning about the holiday as part of a theme unit.

1. Mini-posters with lists of seven personal goals for the coming year. If students are giving the lists to loved ones, the goals may be home-centered (i.e., I will respect my parents). If the students are not bringing the lists home, the goals may be school-centered (i.e., I will read every day).
2. A window box or personally-decorated planter with seedlings.
3. An original poem for a parent, friend, classmate, or neighbor. Help children come up with a list of words they can use, such as the Swahili names of Kwanzaa symbols and their English translations.
4. A note promising to do one chore a day for a week (or more!) at home or at school.
5. A Unity Cup.
6. A mkeka mat for everyone in their family.
7. A family memory scrap book.

Heroes and Role Models

Children can learn about the seven principles by hearing about people who exemplified them. Here is a highly arbitrary list of historic figures. Make this a year-long project and invite children to continue adding contemporary names.

UNITY
Dr. Martin Luther King, Jr., leader of peaceful protests for equal rights.

SELF-DETERMINATION
Rosa Parks, seamstress who decided she should sit where she wanted on public buses and set in motion a civil rights revolution.

COLLECTIVE WORK & RESPONSIBILITY
Thurgood Marshall, first black U.S. Supreme Court justice.

COOPERATIVE ECONOMICS
George Washington Carver, inventor

PURPOSE
A. Philip Randolph, founder of the first black trade union. It won better working conditions for people who worked on railroads.

CREATIVITY
Marian Anderson, singer
Duke Ellington, composer
Jacob Lawrence, painter

FAITH
Each of the people above overcame great obstacles. As you help your students learn more about them, discuss the difficulties they faced and how they overcame them.

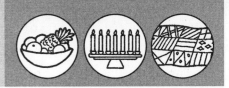

Make a Unity Cup

During Kwanzaa, people sip from a special Unity Cup. Have students make their own unity cups. First, spread a thin layer of glue onto a paper or disposable plastic cup (glue sticks work well for this step). Then wrap red, black, and green yarn around the cup and allow time for the glue to dry. If students celebrate Kwanzaa at home, these make thoughtful gifts for parents or other family members.

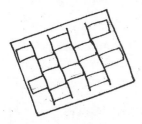

Make a Mkeka

A mkeka is a mat that is placed on the table during the Kwanzaa celebration. The unity cup and basket of fruits and vegetables are placed atop this special mat. It can be made of cloth, straw, or paper, and is often black, red, and green. Your students can follow these simple directions to construct colorful woven mkeka mats of their own. When the mats are complete, display them in your classroom or use them during your Kwanzaa celebration (they make ideal place mats when serving Liberation Rice; find the recipe on page 89). You can also send the mats home for students to give to family members as Kwanzaa gifts.

HOW TO MAKE A MKEKA

You Will Need:
* black, red, and green construction paper
* scissors * tape or glue

1. Fold a piece of black construction paper in half lengthwise

2. Cut slits into the folded edge of the paper. Make the slits about two inches apart. End the slits an inch from the paper's edge. Do NOT cut all the way across.

3. Cut red and green construction paper into strips. Each strip should be about one inch wide and 11 inches long.

4. Weave a strip of red paper through the slits in an over, under, over, under pattern. Repeat with a strip of green paper and reverse the weave.

5. Repeat step four with alternating strips of red and green paper until the woven mat is complete. If you'd like, tape or glue the ends of the strips to the black paper.

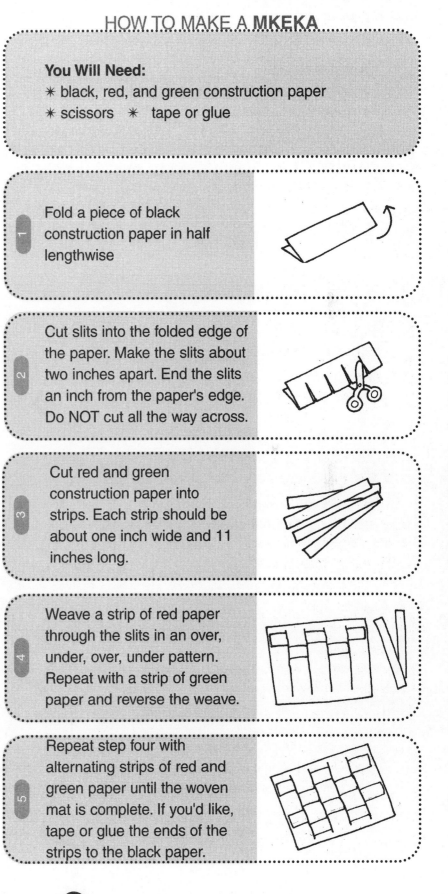

HOW TO MAKE A FAMILY SCRAPBOOK

You Will Need:
* double-sided copies of pages 79-82
* crayons or markers

1. Copy the reproducible pages 79-80 and 81-82 on standard 8.5" x 11" paper. Make the pages double-sided.

2. Fold the front cover/back cover in half along the dotted line.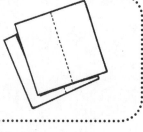

3. Fold the inner pages in half along the dotted line.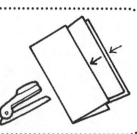

4. Place the inner pages inside the cover, keeping the page numbers in correct order. Staple the edge to bind the book.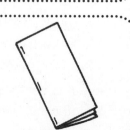

5. Have students complete each page by describing and/or illustrating special family memories. (Each page has a specific prompt for students to follow.)

Family Scrap Book

(Use with the reproducibles on pages 79-82.)

Kwanzaa is a time to celebrate family unity. In fact, many families set aside time during the week to share special memories, honor their ancestors, and applaud the accomplishments of family members young and old. Encourage students to celebrate their own families by making family mini-books. If you'd like, help students assemble the books at school, then send the books home for students and families to fill in and illustrate together.

All Kinds of Kinaras

(Use with the reproducible on page 83.)

A kinara is a special candle holder used during Kwanzaa. It holds seven candles: three red, one black, and three green, in that order. Kwanzaa celebrants light one candle each night of the festival, starting with the black candle in the center. Students may enjoy making or coloring kinaras for your classroom. Here are some ways to use the kinara pattern found on page 83.

Color-by-Numbers Kinara

You Will Need:
* copies of page 83
* black, green, red, brown, and yellow markers or crayons

Lessons & Activities

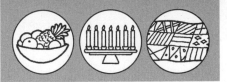

What To Do:

1. Distribute the reproducible to students. Explain that the picture is a kinara, a special candle holder used during Kwanzaa.

2. Point out the numbers in each part of the picture. Explain that students will use those numbers to learn which color to use for each part of the kinara. Show students how to read the Color Box.

3. Allow time for students to color the kinara. When they have finished, you may wish to discuss the symbolism of the colors black, red, and green. (According to Dr. Karenga, the founder of Kwanzaa, black stands for the faces of African-American people; red stood for the blood African-Americans have shed in their struggle for equality; and green for hope and the African homeland.)

Tahira's Felt Kinara

Project contributed by Denise and John Walcott-Christian and their daughter Tahira.

You Will Need:

✳ piece of felt big enough for a wall hanging
✳ Kwanzaa kinara pattern, such as the one on page 83. You can
   make it larger on a copy machine, then trace the bottom of it onto felt.
✳ felt or fabric "candles" (one black, three red, three green)
✳ Velcro-back yellow or orange felt in the shape of flames

What to Do

1. Glue the kinara and the candles to the felt backing. Display the kinara in a prominent spot in the classroom.

2. On each day of Kwanzaa, have students "light" the correct number of candles by placing the "flames" on top. Start with the black candle in the center, then move from left to right.

Celebrate Dreams

(Use with the reproducible on page 84.)

Langston Hughes was a talented and inspirational African-American poet. Read aloud his poem "Dreams" found on page 84. This beautiful poem reflects the Kwanzaa principle of creativity. It also

emphasizes that individuals should reach for and believe in their goals, reflecting the Kwanzaa principles of self-determination, purpose, and faith. After reading the poem, discuss it with your class. Ask: What is a dream? What is your dream for the future? (You may need to point out that our dreams for the future are different from the dreams we have while sleeping at night!) Distribute copies of the poem and invite students to illustrate their own dreams on the other side of the paper.

Where Is Africa?

Most young children do not have a sense of where Africa is located. In addition, many believe that Africa is a country like the United States, and are unaware that it is actually a huge continent containing dozens of countries. Use a globe or world map to show your class where Africa and the United States are located. Then share the following facts about Africa:

✳ Africa contains 53 countries, more than any other continent.

✳ It is the world's second-largest continent, after Asia.

✳ More than 1,000 languages are spoken in Africa.

✳ Africa has many types of landscape, including rain forest, desert, and grasslands.

✳ Some parts of Africa get more than 100 inches of rain each year. In other parts of the continent, rain may not fall for many years.

✳ Africa is home to many kinds of wildlife, including lions, elephants, giraffes, gorillas, and crocodiles.

✳ Africa has many modern cities.

No Water for Hare: An African Folk Tale about Working Together

(Use with reproducibles on pages 85-87.)

Many families enjoy sharing stories at Kwanzaa—especially stories with morals or lessons related to the seven principles of Kwanzaa. The folk tale on pages 85-87 explores the Kwanzaa principle of collective work and responsibility. This Nigerian story is about a group of animals that work together to dig a water hole—and then all enjoy the end result: fresh drinking water. The lazy Hare, who refuses to join in the work, is unable to share in the reward. Read the tale aloud to your students, then discuss it as a class. You might ask:

✳ Why do you think Tortoise called a meeting of the animals? Why didn't he dig the water hole all by himself? (The job was too big for one animal. The animals had to work together.)

✳ How do you think the other animals felt about Hare?

✳ Can you think of a time when we as a class (or you and your friends) worked together to get something done? How did you feel when the job was finished?

Reproduce the stick puppet patterns on page 88 for each child. Have children color, cut out, and glue a craft or Popsicle stick. Read the story again. Invite children to chime in as each animal speaks—and hold up their puppets for the animal that is speaking.

Food for a Feast

(Use with the reproducible on page 89.)

Food is an essential part of any Kwanzaa celebration. Because the holiday recalls traditional harvest festivals, Kwanzaa tables are laden with fruits and vegetables. Families also share a delicious Kwanzaa feast on December 31. You may wish to prepare one or more Kwanzaa dishes for your students to sample. On page 89 you will find a recipe for Gwen's "Liberation Rice," a dish named for the colors of the African liberation flag, which is red, green, and black. Even if you cannot prepare the dish, make copies of the recipe for students to take home. Invite children to design a decorative border for the recipe page.

Other Fun Foods for Kwanzaa

Sesame cookies or crackers
the sesame seed originated in Africa

Yam or sweet-potato chips
buy at a grocery store, or make yourself by thinly slicing sweet potatoes, then frying the slices in vegetable or peanut oil

Corn Graph

During Kwanzaa, a family decorates its table with one ear of corn for each child in the family. (Families with no children often place an ear of corn on the table to represent future offspring or the children of the community.) Explain this tradition to your class and bring in an ear of dried corn for students to see and touch. Then ask students to count the number of children in their own families and figure out how many ears of corn they would need for their tables. Create a simple pictograph or bar graph on the board illustrating the number of children in students' families.

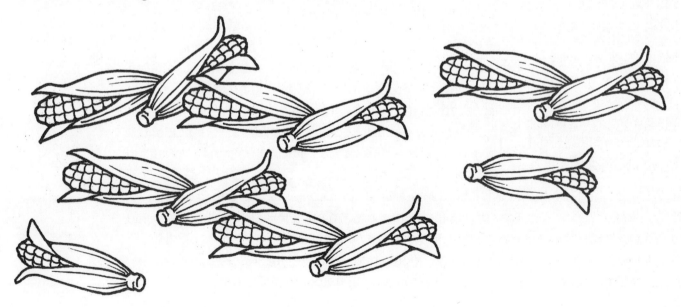

Joyful Sounds

For many celebrants, music is an essential part of the Kwanzaa celebration. Some families sing songs composed by African slaves in the American South, "spirituals" that have special resonance. The spirituals are based on Bible stories and portray a longing for freedom and an end to suffering.

The Kwanzaa Song

Kwanzaa is a hol-i-day.

Kwanzaa is an African hol-i-day.

Seven prin-ci-ples, Seven Candles

Seven days we cel-e-brate.

Some families have their own songs. Here's a song for which you can create your own melody and movements. You can also dance to it, sing in rounds, or sing with a leader. If you have a leader, he or she can clap at different speeds, which the singers have to follow. You can also change the melody from year to year. However it's performed, the Kwanzaa Song definitely creates a joyful sound.

Kwanzaa Paper Dolls

(Use with the reproducibles on pages 90 and 91.)

Many Kwanzaa celebrants choose to wear traditional African attire. Women and girls may wear bright, loose-fitting dresses called *lappas* or *bubas*. Men and boys wear colorful robes called *dashikis* and hats called *kofis*. Everyone in the family may wear beautiful beaded necklaces. Your students can explore traditional Kwanzaa garb by coloring and cutting out the paper dolls and clothes on pages 90 and 91. Provide students with several copies of the pages so that they can color more than one outfit for each doll. Point out to students that traditional African clothes are very colorful, often sporting bright shades of red, yellow, green, or purple. You can also introduce the names of the garments.

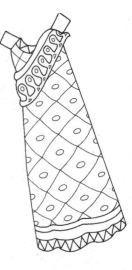

8

Ask the people in your family to sign their names on this page!

1

By _____

My Family Scrapbook

We help each other.
I help my family by

7

There are

people in my family. Their names are

2

One holiday we celebrate is

6

We go places together. Once we went to

3

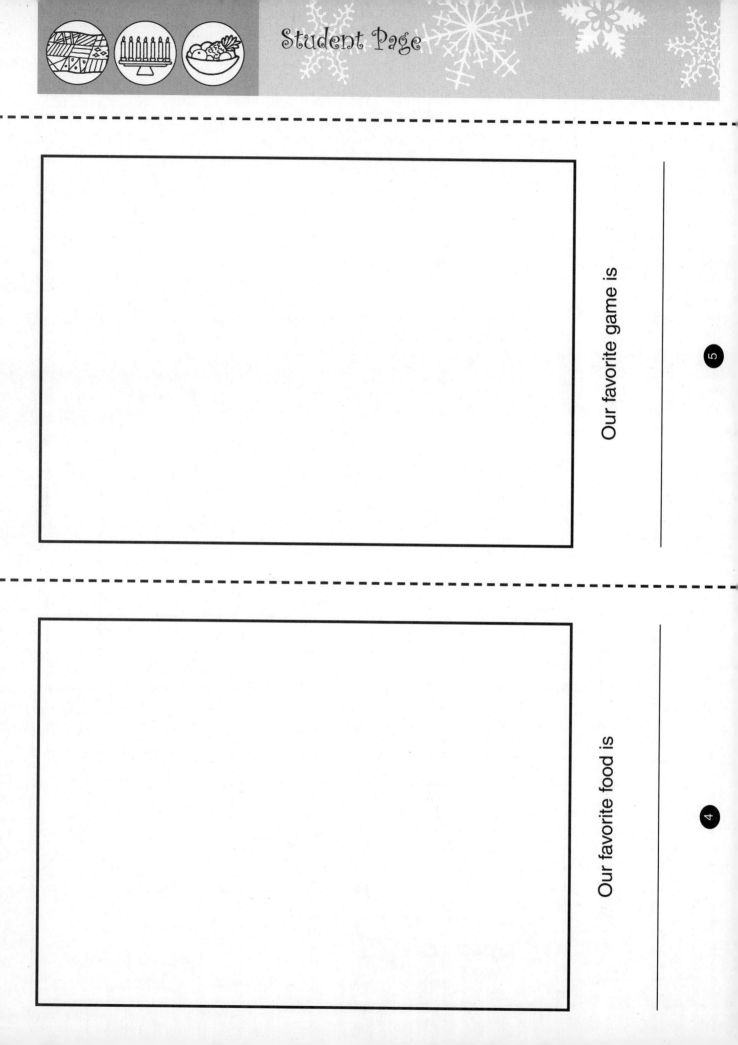

Our favorite game is

5

Our favorite food is

4

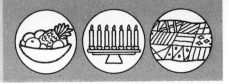

Name _____

Color-by-Numbers Kinara

Look at the number in each part of the picture.
Use the Color Box to find out which color to use.

Color Box: 1. Red   2. Green   3. Black   4. Brown   5. Yellow

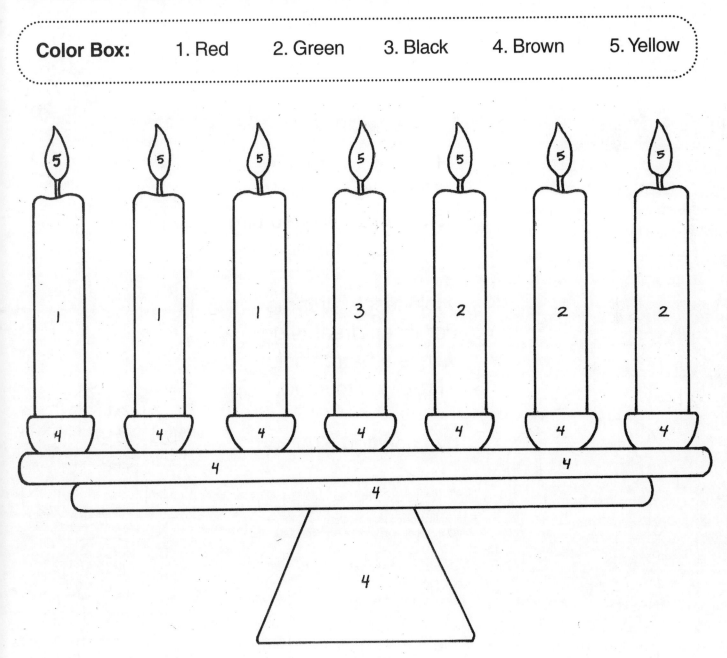

Name _____

Dreams

Hold fast to dreams
For if dreams die
Life is a broken-winged bird
That cannot fly.

Hold fast to dreams
For when dreams go
Life is a barren field
Frozen with snow.

by Langston Hughes

No Water for Hare: A Folktale from Africa

Characters:

Tortoise   Elephant   Snake   Aardvark   Hare

There had been no rain in Africa a very long time, and the creatures of the plains

were thirsty. One day, 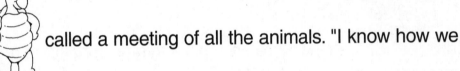 called a meeting of all the animals. "I know how we

can get water," he said. "There is a spring deep in the ground. If we can reach the

spring, we will have all the water we can drink. Now who will help me dig?"

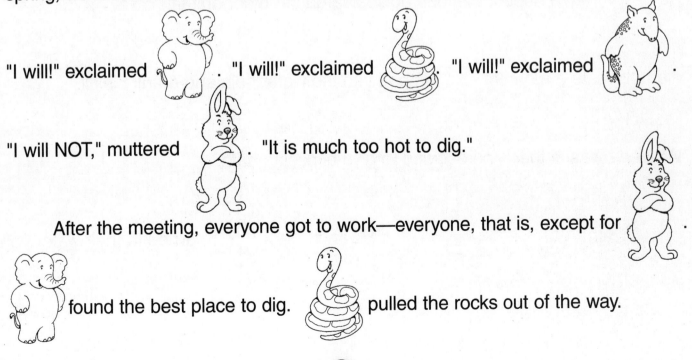

"I will!" exclaimed   . "I will!" exclaimed   . "I will!" exclaimed   .

"I will NOT," muttered   . "It is much too hot to dig."

After the meeting, everyone got to work—everyone, that is, except for   .

    found the best place to dig.   pulled the rocks out of the way.

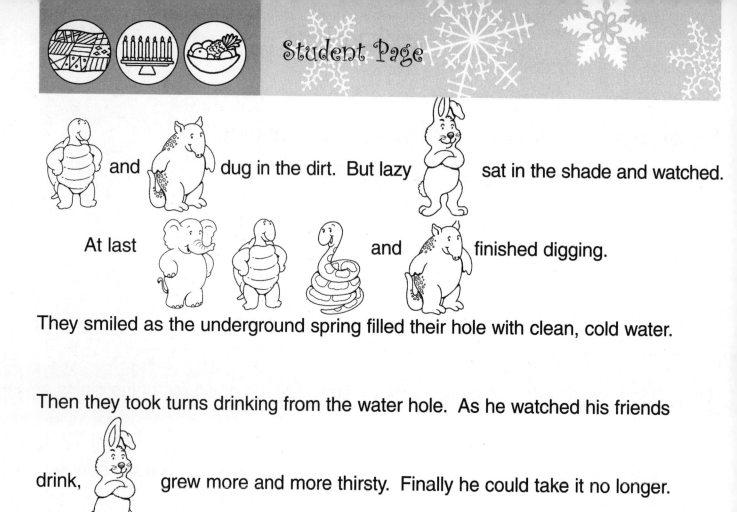

and ___ dug in the dirt. But lazy ___ sat in the shade and watched.

At last ___ ___ ___ and ___ finished digging.

They smiled as the underground spring filled their hole with clean, cold water.

Then they took turns drinking from the water hole. As he watched his friends

drink, ___ grew more and more thirsty. Finally he could take it no longer.

He jumped to his feet, yelling and banging a stick on a gourd.

As ___ had hoped, the loud noise scared the other animals away. ___

did not waste a moment. He jumped into the water hole and drank his fill.

While he was in there, he decided to give himself a bath.

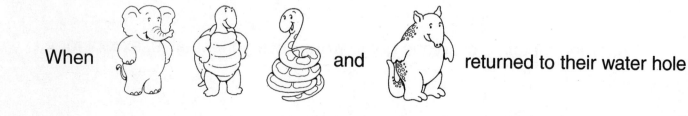

When ___ ___ ___ and ___ returned to their water hole

the next day, they saw the dirty water and knew that 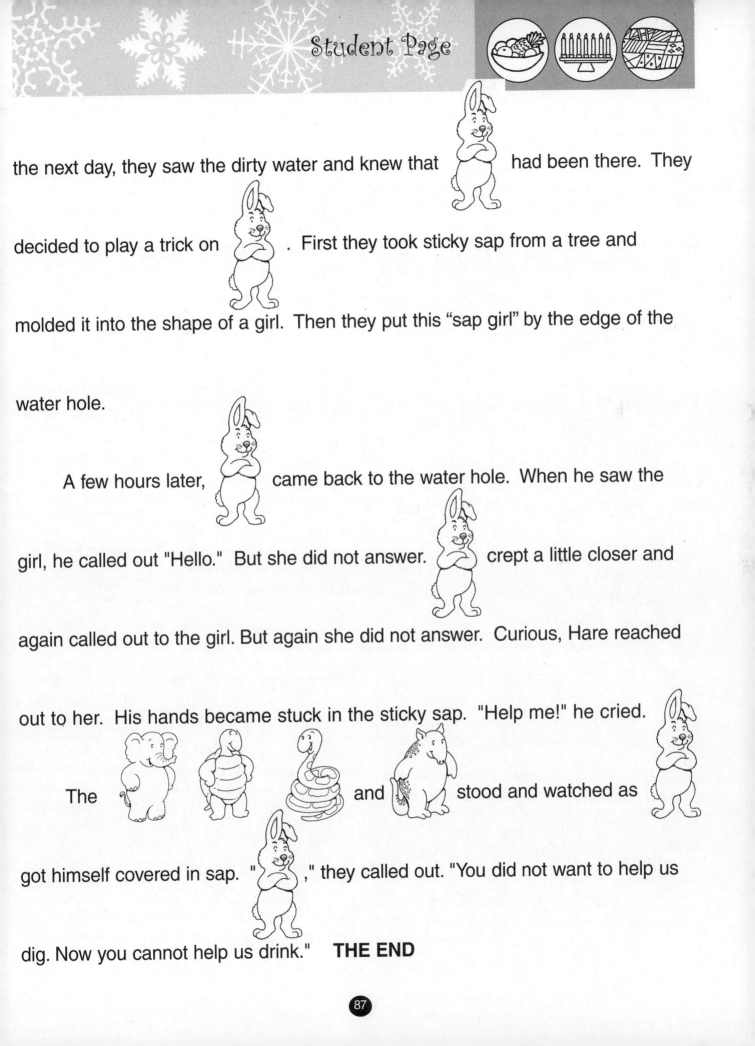 had been there. They

decided to play a trick on 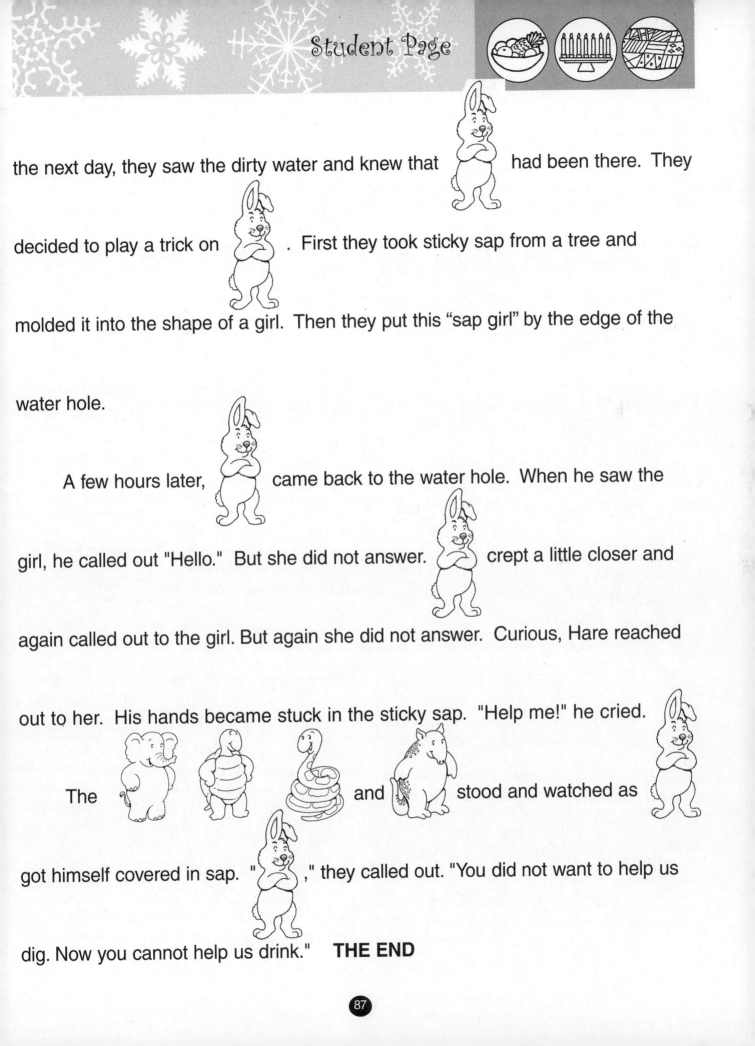. First they took sticky sap from a tree and

molded it into the shape of a girl. Then they put this "sap girl" by the edge of the

water hole.

A few hours later, 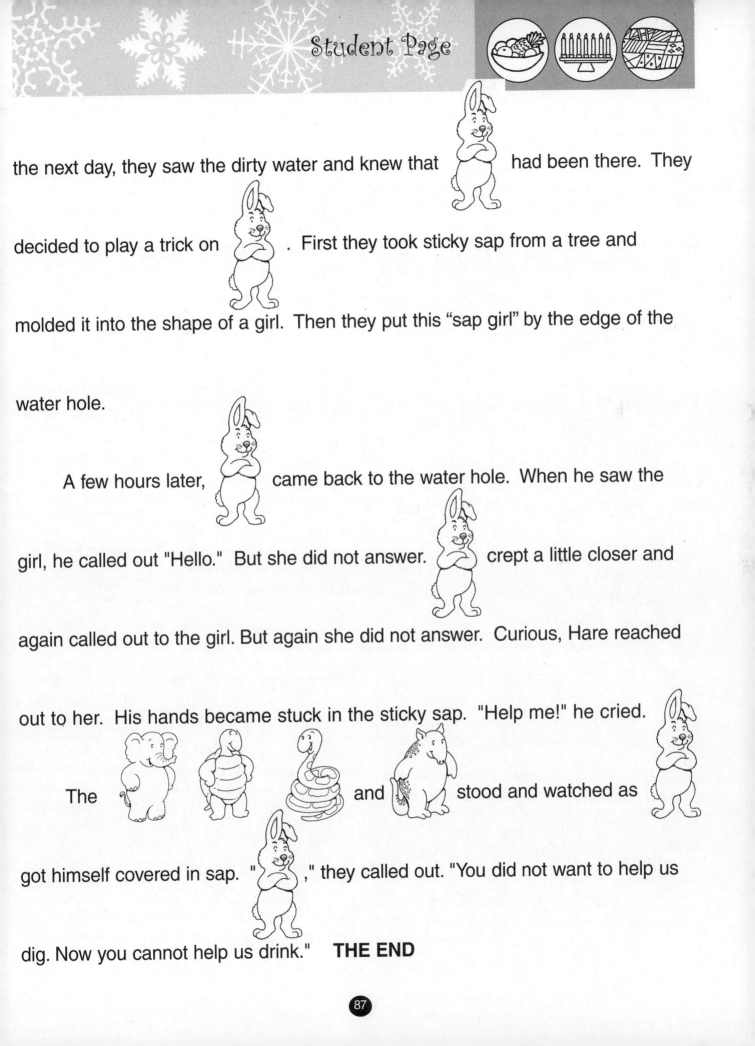 came back to the water hole. When he saw the

girl, he called out "Hello." But she did not answer. 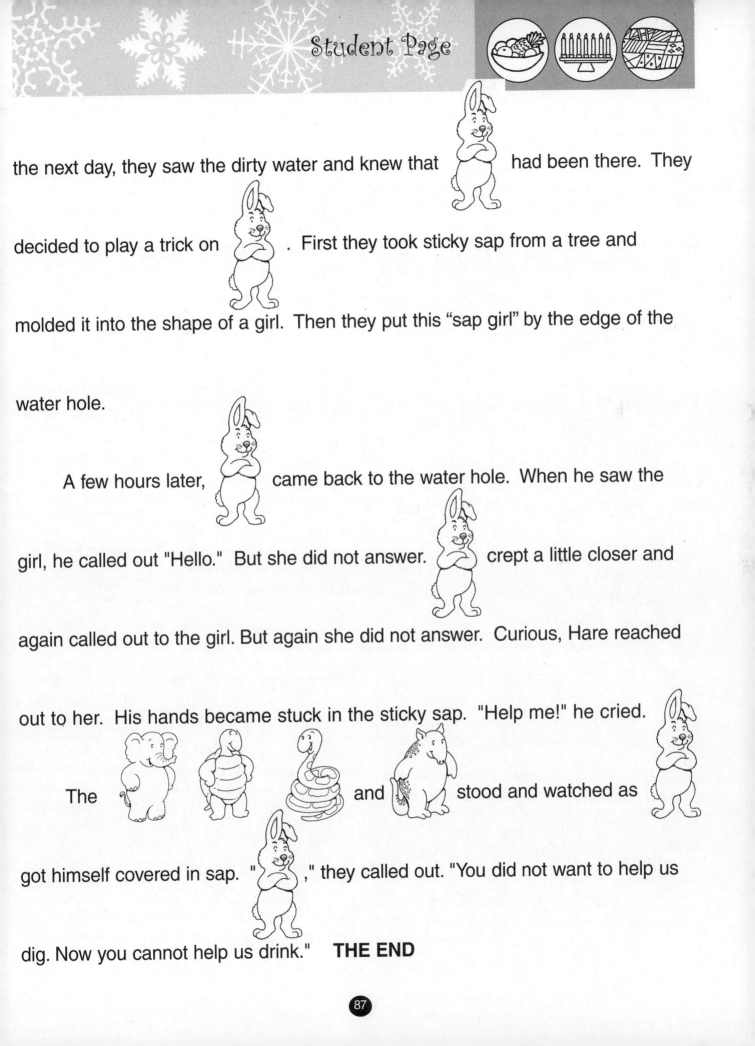 crept a little closer and

again called out to the girl. But again she did not answer. Curious, Hare reached

out to her. His hands became stuck in the sticky sap. "Help me!" he cried.

The 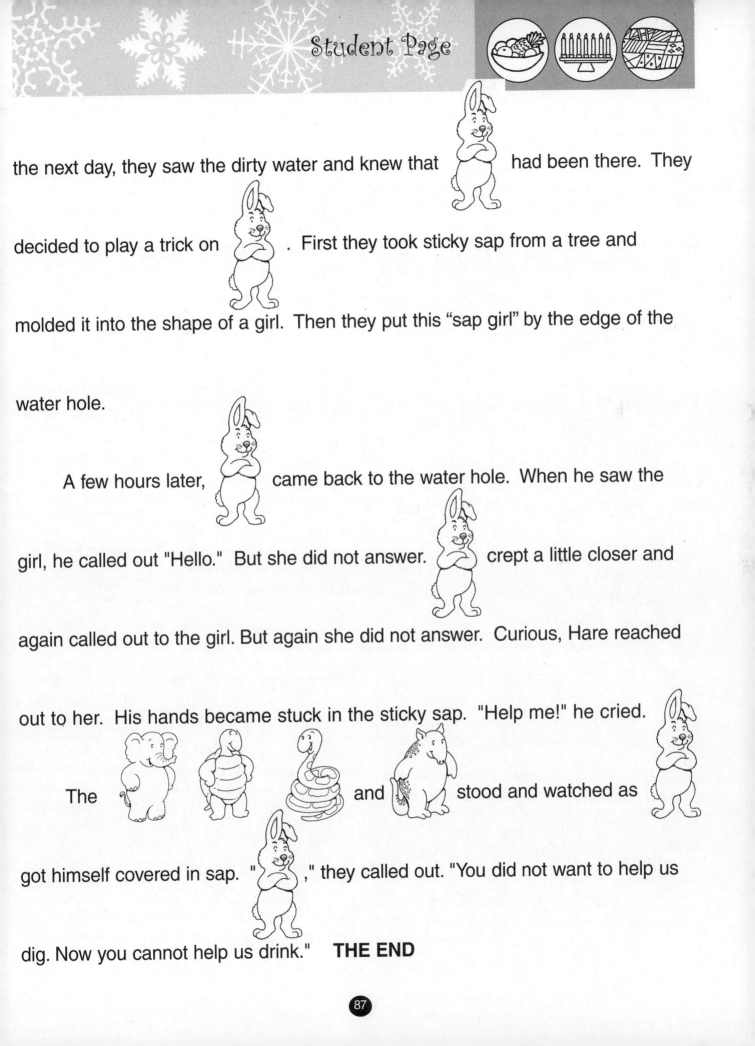 and 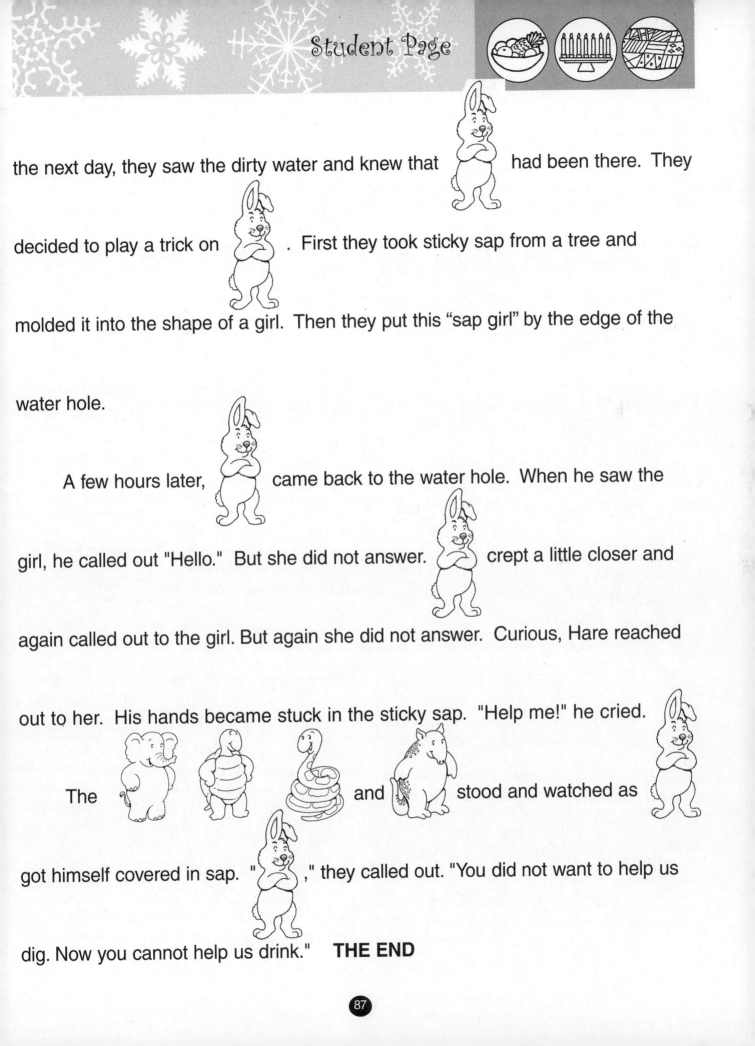 stood and watched as

got himself covered in sap. "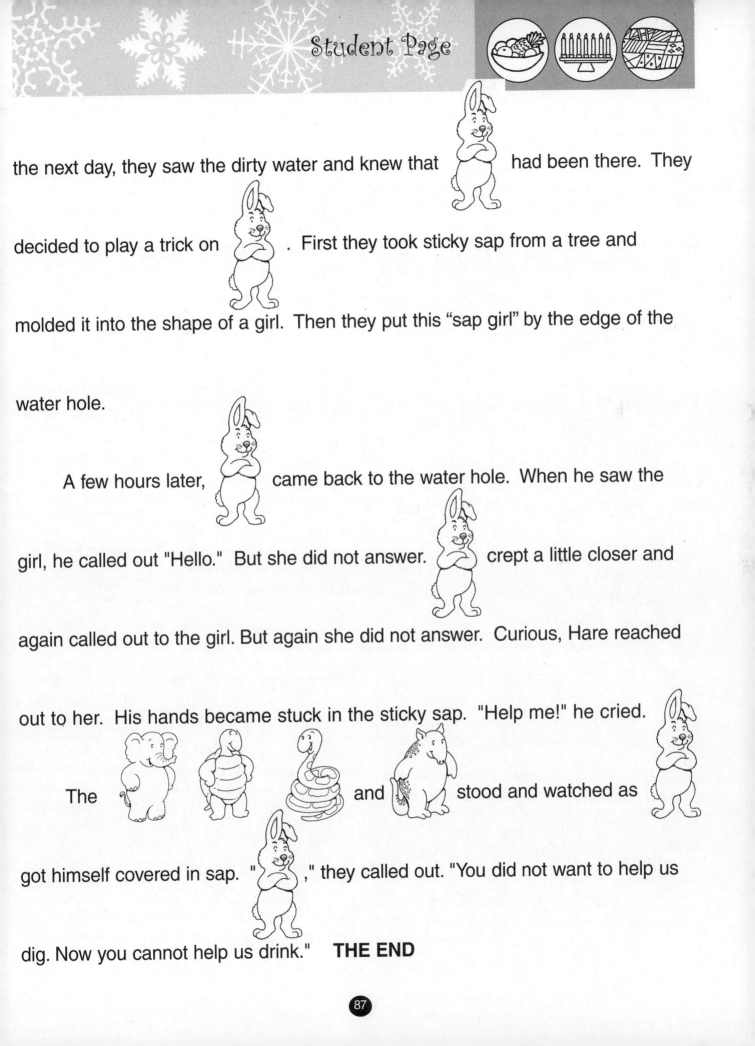," they called out. "You did not want to help us

dig. Now you cannot help us drink." **THE END**

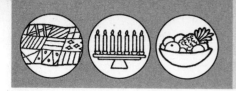

Name _____

Stick Puppets: From the Folktale No Water for Hare

Color and cut out the patterns and glue to the backs of craft or Popsicle sticks.
Use the patterns to act out the folktale.

Name _____

Gwen's Liberation Rice

You Will Need:

* 1 cup of brown rice

* 2 1/4 cups of water

* 1 medium green bell pepper

* 1 can of sliced black olives

* 1 jar of sliced pimentos

* 2 tablespoons of olive oil

* salt to taste

What to Do:

(Children should ask for a grown-up's help.)

1. Chop the pepper.

2. With a grown-up's help, boil the rice until tender, or microwave it.

3. Mix the olive oil with the rice. Stir in the other ingredients.

4. Season with salt.

5. Enjoy!

Name _____

Kwanzaa Paper Dolls

Color and cut out the boy and his clothes. Put the clothes on the boy.

Name _____

Kwanzaa Paper Dolls

Color and cut out the girl and her clothes. Put the clothes on the girl.

Books for Children

Celebrating Kwanzaa, by Diane Hoyt-Goldsmith with photographs by Lawrence Migdale (Holiday House, 1993).
Lawerence Migdale's photos of Kwanzaa rituals help to bring the book to life for young students.

The Children's Book of Kwanzaa: A Guide to Celebrating the Holiday, by Dolores Johnson (Atheneum Books for Young Readers, 1996).
Here's an overview that includes recipes, crafts, special programs, and a clear explanation of the holiday and its significance.

It's Kwanzaa Time!, by Linda and Clay Goss (Philomel, 1995).
The highlight of this book, which you can read aloud, is the section of seven moral tales, one for each of Kwanzaa's seven principles.

My First Kwanzaa Book, by Deborah M. Newton Chocolate with illustrations by Cal Massey (Scholastic, 1992).
Perfect for early readers, this book is a great introduction to Kwanzaa.

Seven Candles for Kwanzaa, by Andrea Davis Pinkney with illustrations by Brian Pinkney (Dial Books for Young Readers, 1993).
An easy-to-read introduction with warm and inviting art of a family getting ready for and then celebrating the holiday.

Books for Adults

Kwanzaa: A Celebration of Family, Community, and Culture, by Dr. Maulana Karenga (University of Sankore Press, Los Angeles, 1989).
The holiday's founder gives an in-depth explanation perfect for educators and parents.

Kwanzaa and Me: A Teacher's Story, by Vivian Gussen-Paley (Harvard University Press, 1996).
In her usual warm writing style, Gussen-Paley tells how she sought to give her students a positive and hopeful view of African-American history.

Web Sites

www.kidsdomain.com/holiday/kwanzaa/index.html
Find online Kwanzaa games, coloring pages, clip art, and more.

www.billybear4kids.com/holidays/kwanzaa/kwanzaa.htm
A kid-friendly site where students can learn about Kwanzaa, make a Kwanzaa calendar, and create bookmarks and other homemade gifts.

The Story of Chinese New Year

Chinese New Year has been celebrated for more than 4,000 years. In ancient China, the New Year celebration was probably held at various times, at the whim of the emperor. Today, the celebration starts on the first day of the Chinese calendar. Because the Chinese calendar is tied to the cycles of the moon, the Chinese New Year is also called the Lunar New Year. The celebration typically falls sometime between late January and mid-February.

Chinese New Year is a holiday rich in symbolism, both religious and cultural. To prepare for the New Year, Chinese people clean their homes from top to bottom, pay off their debts, resolve disagreements, and buy new clothes and shoes. This period of preparation is known as the "Little New Year" and is meant to chase away the evil influences of the year that is coming to an end. And it's no good putting it off. The Chinese believe that those who wait until New Year's Day to clean, also sweep away the good fortune about to come!

On the night before the New Year begins, Chinese families gather to feast on "lucky" foods such as mandarin cakes (symbolizing fulfilled wishes), shrimp (symbolizing wealth), and puffed rice cakes (symbolizing a sweet New Year). They visit cemeteries to honor their ancestors and set up altars with pictures of deceased relatives. On this night, Chinese children try to stay up as late as they can; it is believed that the longer they can stay awake, the longer their parents' lives will be.

On the first day of the New Year, people dress in their best clothes and visit friends and relatives. No work is done on New Year's Day because it is believed that working on this special day will lead to hard work all year long. On this day, children are given red envelopes full of money, called *li-shih*. People decorate their homes with red banners featuring messages of luck and happiness. Lion Dancers perform in front of businesses—for a donation—to bestow good luck on those inside. The New Year celebration continues until the moon is full. Then, festivities come to a close with the great Festival of Lanterns. The streets are filled with the noise and excitement of a giant parade led by a huge dragon. People carrying lanterns join the parade, and fireworks are set off to scare away evil spirits. Today the Chinese New Year is celebrated not just in China, but in many cities worldwide. People in Korea, Tibet, and Vietnam also celebrate variations of the Lunar New Year.

The date for Chinese New Year varies from year to year. Here's a peek at the dates for the next few years: February 12, 2002; February 1, 2003; January 22, 2004; February 9, 2005; January 29, 2006; February 18, 2007.

Gung Hay Fat Choy! Bai-nien! May you prosper! Happy New Year!

Some Symbols of Chinese New Year

Many people decorate their homes with flower buds just ready to open. It's believed that if the buds open on New Year's day, they will bring good luck.

Fruits and other foods have great symbolism during the New Year. Peaches signify immortality. Oranges and melons stand for the moon, a lucky omen. But if you're given an orange on the first day of the new year, wait until the second day of the year to eat it—or it will bring bad luck.

Chinese households display red banners with special sayings during the New Year celebration. These sayings, called *fai chun*, are written in Chinese characters. They are meant to wish good luck and prosperity to friends and passersby.

The dragon, which is a traditional part of the New Year's parade, symbolizes strength and luck.

The Chinese animal zodiac is an important part of the New Year remembrance. Each year is named after an animal which has certain characteristics. It is said that people born during that year will have those same traits. There are 12 animals in the Chinese zodiac: rat, ox, tiger, rabbit, dragon, snake, horse, goat, monkey, rooster, dog, pig.

The fireworks that light up the streets during the Chinese New Year symbolize the banishing of bad luck.

Lion and Dragon Masks

(Use with the reproducibles on pages 100-101.)

Chinese-American communities in the United States often hold colorful parades to usher in their New Year. A traditional part of the parade is the dragon—a colorful paper costume held up by several dancers. The dragon twists and turns as the dancers move. Hundreds of years ago, dragons symbolized the Chinese emperors and were greatly feared. Another part of the festivities is the Lion Dance, performed by people inside a fierce lion costume. Both dances are performed to the beat of a large, loud drum. The lion and the dragon are meant to frighten away evil spirits.

You can recreate the festive atmosphere of a New Year's parade by making your own lion and dragon masks. When you have finished, let students wave the masks as they parade around your school. You can designate one or more students to be the drummer(s).

You Will Need:
* copies of page 100 and 101 * paper plates * craft sticks or Popsicle sticks
* markers or crayons * glitter, yarn, and other decorative materials * glue

What to Do:
1. Let children decide which animal they'd like to make. Distribute one reproducible to each student, and allow time for them to color the pictures.
2. Cut out each design and glue it onto the raised side of a paper plate.
3. Add bits of bright yarn, glitter, or other art materials to make the animals more exciting-looking.
4. Glue a craft stick onto the bottom of each paper plate. You may wish to use heavy masking tape to help the art stick stay in place.
5. Show students how to use the stick to raise and lower the mask.

Banners of Good Wishes

(Use with the reproducible on page 102.)

During the Chinese New Year, people hang long, red banners with special phrases near their doorways. The phrases are written vertically in Chinese characters. Some popular phrases include:

Dazhan hongtu (May you realize your ambitions.)

Wanshi ruyi (May all your wishes be granted.)

Gung hay fat choy (Prosperous and happy new year.)

Invite children to make their own banners to hang on their desks or bedroom doorknobs. Reproduce and distribute the Banner of Good Wishes pattern on page 102 to each child. Read the English phrases out loud. Then help children color the patterns red and cut them out. Have children glue the patterns on to a larger sheet of red construction paper. Finally, supply gold glitter or strips of gold paper to decorate the banners.

A teacher, student, or local merchant who speaks and writes a Chinese dialect may be able to assist you. You can also make copies of the common New Year greetings on page 102 and have students copy these. If you'd like, make larger banners to hang on your classroom door.

Precious Red Envelopes

One of the many reasons Chinese children have such an affinity for this holiday is that parents are not supposed to scold them! And, on New Year's Day, children are given red envelopes filled with money for luck and prosperity. This gesture is called *lai see* or *li-shih* in Cantonese and *hongbao* in Mandarin.

Students can make their own *li-shih* envelopes out of red construction paper. Give each student half of one piece of paper (each student will need a piece about 9" x 6"). Fold that piece in half again and staple the two sides closed, leaving the top open to create a pouch. Now decorate the front of each pouch with greetings and good wishes for the New Year.

Instead of putting money in their envelopes, students can write special messages of good luck to a friend or family member and present the envelope as a unique gift.

Nian, The Dragon: A Classroom Mini-Play

(Use with the reproducibles on pages 103-106.)

Here's a Chinese New Year treat, the adaptation of a folk tale that your students and some helpers can present to the school. Ask two older students from another class or two of your class parents to read this story aloud as your children mime it. See page 103 for a list of fun props children can use for their performance.

Go Fly a Kite!

Colorful kites are often seen at New Year's celebrations. Kites have a long history in China. Thousands of years ago, Chinese war lords and emperors used kites to scare away enemies. These earliest kites were made of bamboo. As they flew in the wind, they made an eerie sound that some warriors thought were messages from the gods warning them of awful things to come. The kites were called *feng cheng*, or wind harps.

Make your own decorative diamond-shaped kites out of construction paper, tissue paper, drinking straws, string, and other everyday materials. Or, log on to www.sound.net/~kiteguy/littlekids/littlekids.htm for directions on making simple sky-worthy models. Decorate your room with kites for the New Year or use them to decorate a Happy Chinese New Year bulletin board.

Book Link

Meet a Lion Dancer!
Grab students' attention by letting them experience the Chinese New Year through the eyes of a boy their own age! Read aloud *Lion Dancer: Ernie Wan's Chinese New Year* by Kate Waters and Madeline Slovenz-Low (Scholastic, 1990). The book tells the story of 6-year-old Ernie, who is preparing for his first public performance of the special Lion Dance. After reading, discuss the story. Ask: Why do you think Ernie has been practicing so hard? How do you think he feels as he gets ready for the Lion Dance? Have you ever been nervous about something? How did it turn out?

Festive Foods

(Use with the reproducible on page 107.)

Don't forget to take a snack break during your study of Chinese New Year! Most Chinese families enjoy dried oysters, seaweed, boiled dumplings (*po-po*), and pastries called moon cakes during the holiday. They also eat a variety of fruits, each one symbolizing prosperity, good luck, or some other good wish for the year ahead. Although many traditional Chinese dishes are elaborate and difficult to make in a school setting, a colorful fruit salad featuring many symbolic fruits is tasty, nutritious, and easy to prepare!

Use the reproducible on page 107 to prepare the lucky fruit salad. Then, as students sample the dish, explain the symbolism of each type of fruit:

Fruit	Meaning
Melon	wealth, virtue, and good health
Persimmons or Apples	fulfilled wishes
Peaches	immortality or long life
Oranges	money
Tangerines	good luck

On the day that you serve the fruit, decorate your classroom to look like a Chinese marketplace. Ask each child to bring in a flower—real or paper. Arrange the flowers on a table, along with whole melons, persimmons or apples, oranges, tangerines, and peaches. Make a sign that says *hung fa gi*. This means "flower street" in Chinese and is the traditional name for the marketplace where shoppers buy flowers and fruit.

Happy Chinese New Year (A Poem)
(Use with the reproducible on page 108.)

Helen Moore's poem, "Happy Chinese New Year," reflects the vibrance and excitement of the holiday. Read the poem aloud several times to your class. Then, distribute copies of the poem and have students draw decorative borders for the page using Chinese New Year symbols such as dragons, lions, fruits, and flower blossoms. Encourage students to use "fiery" colors such as red and yellow.

Where Is China?

Although Chinese New Year is celebrated in cities around the world, some of the biggest and most exciting celebrations are held in mainland China. Use a globe or world map to show students where China is located. Then share these fascinating facts:
* China is the third-largest country in the world, after Canada and Russia.
* One out of every five of the world's people lives in China.
* China has one of the oldest civilizations in the world.
* Long ago, the Chinese people built a gigantic wall to keep their enemies out of their country. It is called the Great Wall, and it's so long it can be seen from the Moon!

Zodiac Parade
(Use with the reproducibles on pages 109 and 110.)

In the Chinese calendar, each year is named for an animal. The year in which a person is born is said to determine the way he or she acts. For example, a person born in the Year of the Dragon would be brave and imaginative. A person born in the Year of the Monkey would be clever and mischievous. People who believe in the zodiac base many of their most important decisions on its guidelines. There are 12 animals

in the zodiac, starting with the rat and ending with the pig. When one cycle of the zodiac ends, a new cycle begins.

In this activity, students will make simple pull-through zodiac charts with just a few cuts and folds.

What's Your Animal?

(Use with the reproducible on page 111.)

Make several copies of the reproducible and distribute them to small groups of children. Help students find the animal for the year they were born, as well as the animals for siblings or friends. With older students, you can play a math game. Ask: "When you are 10 years old, which animal will be the symbol?" and so on. Ask children to consider whether they have their animals' special qualities—or, if not, what animals they do resemble.

HOW TO MAKE A ZODIAC PARADE

You Will Need:
* a copy of page 109 and page 110 for each student
* markers or crayons for coloring
* scissors
* tape

1 Distribute the reproducible pages to each child. On page 110, cut along the solid line. Then fold along the dotted line. Glue the middle, creating a single strip with animals on both sides.

2 On page 109, cut along the solid lines. Then cut out the two small windows. Fold along the dotted lines and tape. You will now have a long sleeve that is open at both ends.

3 Color the animals on the strip and the parade scene on the sleeve.

4 Insert the strip into the sleeve, and pull until an animal and its special quality appear in the windows. Keep pulling to the left until you have seen all six animals. Then turn the strip over.

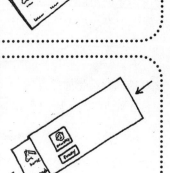

Name _____

Dragon Mask

Name _____

Lion Mask

Name _____

Banner of Good Wishes Pattern

Fooh!

May you have happiness and great fortune!

Gung hay fat choy!

Prosperous and happy new year!

Huang-chin wan-liang!

May you have ten thousand pieces of gold!

Name _____

Nian, The Dragon: A Classroom Play

Props:

✳ Tools villagers can use to look busy

✳ Pot lids to bang together

✳ Foil to make the noise of a crackling bonfire

✳ Colored paper to depict the seasons and the passing of time

✳ Drum with a deep sound

✳ Large sheets of red paper

Characters:

✳ Miguel

✳ Reader 1

✳ Reader 2

✳ Nian, a dragon (roars)

✳ Boy, Girl, and Villagers (mime their parts, but do not speak)

✳ Drummer (drums slowly every time Nian appears)

Reader 1:   Do you know how the Chinese New Year began many thousands of years ago? We know.

Reader 2:   In that long-ago time, when mists swirled over the ancient land of China, there was a village. It was the home of Boy and Girl and they loved it dearly.

[Boy and Girl skip and play. The Villagers work.]

Reader 1:   One full moon passed and then another. Soon it was winter, when the nights seemed far too long and far too dark. Everyone became more careful—and a little bit frightened. One day, the villagers put down their tools. All work stopped. All playing stopped. The people hid inside their homes.

[Villagers hold up dark paper to show winter. Act out going into their homes.]

103

Reader 2:   From their hiding places, the villagers heard a roar.

Reader 1:   It grew louder and louder. Nian was coming.

[Nian roars and clomps about. The drummer drums.]

Reader 2:   The people trembled so much that their houses shook. Nian kept roaring as he looked for something to eat.

[Nian roars and clomps about. The drummer drums.]

Reader 1:   The people knew what would happen if Nian found them. He would have them for dinner! It had happened every year for as long as anyone could remember.

Reader 2:   This kept up for a few days. Finally, Nian left. He was no longer hungry.

Reader 1:   The villagers came out of their homes. They had 11 full moons to be happy. But they knew Nian would be back at the time of the 12th moon.

Reader 2:   Boy and Girl wondered why this kept happening. They asked everyone in the village. But everyone simply shrugged and looked frightened.

[Boy and Girl walk up to several Villagers. The Villagers shrug.]

Reader 1:   Boy and Girl didn't want to spend the rest of their lives hiding from a dragon. So they made a plan.

[Boy and Girl whisper together.]

Reader 2:   When winter came again, the villagers hid in their homes. But not Boy and Girl. They hid behind a cart in the village square.

Reader 1:   From their hiding places, the villagers heard a roar.

Reader 2:   It grew louder and louder.

[Nian roars and clomps about. The drummer drums.]

Reader 1:   The people trembled so much that their houses shook. Nian kept roaring as he looked for something to eat.

[Nian roars and clomps about. The drummer drums.]

Reader 2:   Boy and Girl were very frightened. But they knew they had to go ahead with their plan.

Reader 1:   Nian came closer and closer. Boy and Girl could hear his giant feet hitting the dirt road.

[Nian roars and clomps about. The drummer drums.]

Reader 2: Boy sneezed. Nian heard and headed toward the cart.

Reader 1: Just as Nian came close to them, Boy and Girl jumped out from behind the cart. They held noisemakers. They banged. And they clanged. They made a lot of noise, but then so did the dragon. After a while, Nian began to back away from the village.

Reader 2: The villagers came out of their homes and thanked Boy and Girl. Still, everyone was worried. People had a feeling Nian would return. This time, though, they would be ready.

Reader 1: That night, Nian returned. The people trembled so much that their houses shook.

[Nian roars and clomps about. The drummer drums.]

Reader 1: But all Nian saw was the bright glare of a bonfire the people had built. It crackled. It hissed. It made a lot of noise, but then so did the dragon. But after a while, Nian began to back away from the village.

Reader 2: The people sighed in relief. But Boy and Girl did not believe Nian was gone forever. They had one last idea. The next day the villagers painted their doors bright red.

(Villagers hold up sheets of red paper.]

Reader 1: Nian returned. The villagers could hear his giant feet hitting the dirt road. They stood behind their doors and waited. Would Boy and Girl's plan work?

[Nian roars and clomps about. The drummer drums.]

Reader 1: Nian did not notice the people. All he saw was the red of their doors. Nian turned and began to back away from the village.

Both Readers: And this time Nian was gone for good. The dragon was never seen again—except at parades, when brave girls and boys use noisemakers and firecrackers to keep the dragon in line.

Name _____

Lucky Fruit Salad

You Will Need:

✳ Melon

✳ Persimmons or apples

✳ Peaches

✳ Oranges

✳ Tangerines

What to Do:
(Children should ask for
a grown-up's help.)

1. Cut melon, peaches, and
   persimmons or apples into
   small cubes.

2. Peel citrus fruits and break
   into segments.

3. Toss the fruits together
   in a large bowl.

Name _____

Happy Chinese New Year
"Gung hay fat choy!"

In China every girl and boy
celebrates the New Year
in a very special way—
With fireworks and dragons,
colored red and gold—
They welcome in the new year
and chase away the old!

by Helen Moore

From *Poem A Day* (Scholastic, © 1997)

Name _____

Zodiac Parade Pattern

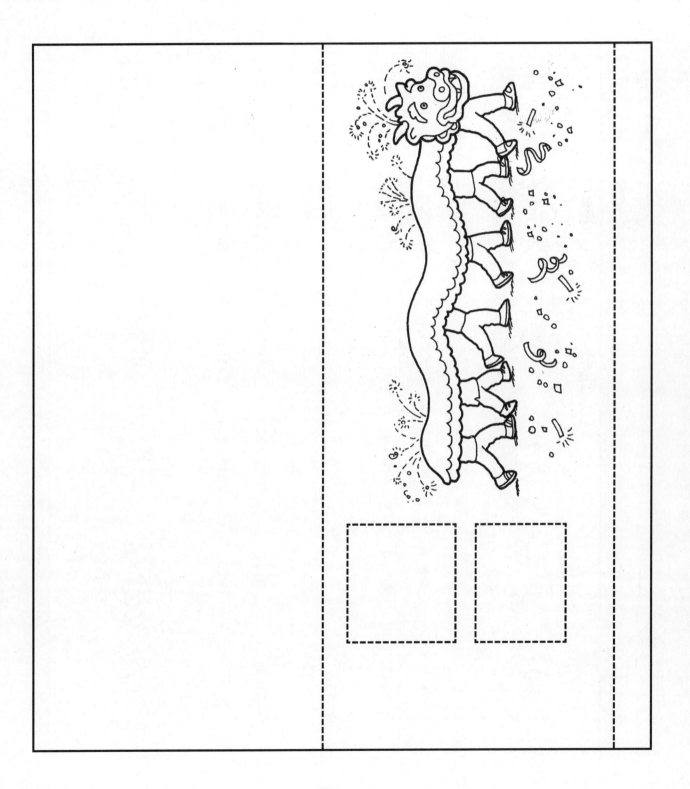

Name _____

Zodiac Parade Pattern

snake	tricky	horse friendly
dragon	strong	sheep creative
rabbit	shy	monkey funny
tiger	brave	rooster popular
ox	gentle	dog loyal
rat	honest	pig caring

Name _____

What's Your Animal?

Find the animal for the year you were born and circle it. Then find the animals for your family and friends!

ANIMAL		PERSONALITY	YEARS
Rat	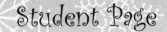	honest, energetic	1984, 1996. 2008
Ox		gentle, peace-loving	1985, 1997, 2009
Tiger		strong, brave	1986, 1998, 2010
Rabbit		shy, clever	1987, 1999, 2011
Dragon		lucky, strong	1988, 2000, 2012
Snake		wise, calm	1989, 2001, 2013
Horse		friendly, athletic	1990, 2002, 2014
Sheep		elegant, creative	1991, 2003, 2015
Monkey		funny, intelligent	1992, 2004, 2016
Rooster		sincere, popular	1993, 2005, 2017
Dog		courageous, loyal	1994, 2006, 2018
Pig		sincere, caring	1995, 2007, 2019

Books for Children

Celebrating Chinese New Year, by Diane
Hoyt-Goldsmith (Holiday House, 1998).
   Ten-year-old Ryan Leong and his family
   celebrate and explain the Chinese
   New Year.

The Chinese New Year, by Cheng Hou-tien
(Holt, Rinehart and Winston, 1976).
   Scissor-cut artwork illustrates this
   introduction to a holiday the author
   celebrated as a boy in Taiwan.

Happy New Year, by June Behrens
(Children's Press, 1982).
   Colorful photos tell about a Golden Dragon
   Parade in a California Chinatown.

Lion Dancer: Ernie Wan's Chinese New Year,
by Kate Waters and Madeline Slovenz-Low
(Scholastic, 1990).
   Martha Cooper's colorful photographs
   illustrate a few days in the life of young
   Ernie Wan as he prepares for the great
   honor of being a lion dancer in New York's
   Chinese New Year parade.

Web Sites

www.chinascape.org/china/culture/holidays/
hyuan/newyear.html
   Find out when Chinese New Year will
   be held each year, how the holiday
   originated, and how it's celebrated.